Celebrity 2.0

Celebrity 2.0

The Role of Social Media Influencer Marketing in Building Brands

Stacy Landreth Grau

BEP

BUSINESS EXPERT PRESS

Leader in applied, concise business books

This book is for my teenage daughters, Ellie and Maddy,
who are content creators in their own right and who taught
me the power of social media for Generation Z

Description

Social media influencers rule the world!

Gone are the days of worshipping movie stars and athletes only for their talent. Everyday people are fast becoming the new celebrities and thus influencers for Millennials and Generation Z. In the past few years, social media influencers dominate pop culture and brands are eager to work with them to build their brands. From music to gaming; from fashion to sports; from wellness to lifestyle branding there are more than 50 million people calling themselves "creators" and many are influencers amassing a highly engaged community. For brands, what are the most effective ways to identify and cultivate influencers and support content creation?

This book is for anyone who wants to understand the landscape of influencer marketing with an eye for collaborations between influencers and companies. Perfect for brand managers and agency professionals, up and coming influencers, and students wanting to enter this exciting field of marketing, this book combines practical advice and examples with an overview of the academic insights to date. Topics include creators and the creator economy, typology of influencers, how to work with them, considerations for campaign design and implementation.

Celebrity 2.0: The Role of Social Media Influencer Marketing to Build Brands is a great primer to the influencer marketing ecosystem and the influencer marketing relationship framework to learn how content marketing, native advertising and content marketing all come together.

Keywords

influencer marketing; social media influencer marketing; influencers; content marketing; native advertising; influencer marketing agencies; influencer marketplaces; authenticity; expertise; trust; source credibility

Contents

Acknowledgments

There are so many to thank. Of course, huge thanks to my husband and daughters for their sincere patience and enthusiasm while I wrote this book especially when they would rather be doing something else. Thanks for support from my parents. Thanks goes out to my friends who reviewed drafts of the chapters (Tracey) and who designed some great visual content (Sydney) and to friends who simply supported me through the journey. Thanks to my Happy Hour crew of Susan, Laura, Jessica, Hettie, and Lynn and my partners at IdeaFactory—Cedric and Trish. To my mentor, Amanda, who started me on this journey 20 years ago and still inspires me to do it. To the patience of the folks at Business Expert Press who were so kind while I worked through this during the pandemic (while teaching a full load at the same time). To the amazing people I talked to on this journey and who I am looking forward to connecting with again. A special shout out to Addi Hall McCauley who really helped me start the ball rolling with this. And last, to all my amazing former students from TCU who were instrumental in getting my interviews. It is astounding what you have all been able to do.

Introduction

Drivers of Influencer Marketing

Launching a New Brand Using Influencers

Can a new brand build its growth and build its brand image using primarily social media influencers (SMI)? New brands come and go and often have a tough time unseating the category leaders, especially in extremely competitive spaces such as beauty and skincare. However, indi skincare brand Tula (which means "balance" in Sanskrit) has been able to increase awareness and sales primarily through building their marketing foundation on authentic social media influencers and paid social advertising boosts. In 2020, the brand—which is based on the intersection of wellness and beauty—garnered $56 million in earned media value. The skincare brand unveiled its #EmbraceYourSkin campaign in October 2020 and reached more than 120 million consumers and recorded more than one million engagements through the end of the year.

Tula (www.tula.com) is a "digitally native and social media first" brand with a majority of its revenue coming from direct to consumers (DTC) with three times revenue growth in the past three years. The brand was first launched in 2014 by Dr. Roshini Raj, a gastroenterologist and internist who focuses on probiotics and superfoods in her practice found the same benefits for skincare. She launched Tula with cofounders Ken Landis, cofounder of Bobbi Brown cosmetics, and Dan Reich, a tech entrepreneur, to maximize the benefits of natural ingredients for skincare for all types of skin issues. In 2017, the company garnered significant capital infusion to scale revenue and growth. In the past two years, Tula has seen several successful product launches. In April 2020, Tula launched a gel sunscreen that was the most requested products from customers and was one of the most successful product launches for them. In October 2020, Tula and gymnast Shawn Johnson partnered in a limited edition So

Pumpkin exfoliating sugar scrub, which sold within hours of its launch. As a result of this launch, Tula earned $6.1 million in earned media value in October alone, ranking number two among skincare brands.

Perhaps, part of it was timing. When the pandemic hit, customers found themselves increasingly concerned about health and wellness (and more people embraced the "no makeup" look since everyone was home). As part of the #EmbraceYourSkin campaign, Tula tapped social media influencers Tess Holliday, Tennille Murphy, Nyma Tang, Chizi Duru, and Weylie Hoang to create kits to address specific skin issues. Interestingly, this stable of influencers was the result of an intentional effort where Tula recruited influencers based on a revenue sharing model similar to Avon. As part of the campaign, influencers interacted with followers using video tutorials and engaging in conversations about skincare. Conversations happened both on Tula's social channels and within influencers' social channels. CEO Savannah Sachs said, "We're proud to shine a spotlight on the work and impact that these women have had in the industry, specifically for ageless and natural beauty, size representation and skin tone diversity."[1]

Why are influencers so effective for Tula? One could argue that Tula was effective at getting attention. Tula was able to capture the attention of enough customers who then made purchases. However, as Amanda Russell argues in her book *The Influencer Code*, "attention is currency, attention is not success. The world is largely confusing attention with influence. Attention without trust is simply noise."[2] It could also be because consumers don't really want to have relationships with brands; rather they are more interested in people. According to Neal Shaffer, author of *The Age of Influence*, "Harnessing true people power—and that is what the voices of influencers are—requires a different approach to how brands traditionally spread their message. It is a shift in communicating and interacting with your customers and audience. It's about user generated content. It's about community. It's about relationships. It's about engagement."[3] As influencer marketing—boosted by social media platforms and technology—increasingly becomes a larger part of a brand's marketing budget, it is important to understand more about it what influencer marketing is, why it works for brands and audiences, and how it works most effectively. To do that, let's start at the foundation.

The Nature of Influence

Social influence is the ways that people change their attitudes, beliefs, or behaviors based on the information and actions of others in order for people to meet the demands of a social environment. Social influence is the foundation for influencer marketing, but social influence is more than just popularity, or "going viral" or being famous.[4] It is a natural process used by other people and businesses to influence a person's attitude and/ or behavior. Social influence drives how effective celebrity endorsers and social media influencers can be in their attempts to persuade others to act (or in the case of marketing—to buy). Social influence can be thought of as the "what" behind influencer marketing. In 1958, psychologist Herbert Kelman identified three broad varieties of social influence (compliance, identification, and internalization). When considering influencer marketing, the conceptualization of identification—when people "wish to establish or maintain a satisfying self-defining relationship to another person or group and he/she adopts the influence because it is associated with the desired relationship"[5]—is one of the critical concepts. Often, these relationships are with someone who is liked and respected. Additionally, informational social influence involves accepting information or advice from a person who may not have previously been known as a friend or colleague, and this theory also helps us to understand the foundations of influencer marketing. Specifically, it sheds light on how a person (e.g., influencer) who is not known personally to people but who have something (e.g., expertise, trust, or other quality) that is compelling enough for people to follow his/her advice and suggestions can be an effective marketing strategy.

Other related theories also provide a strong foundation for influencer marketing. Psychologist Robert Cialdini[6] defined seven principles of persuasion that can contribute to someone's propensity to be influenced. This can get into the mechanics of how the message is constructed. The seven principles include reciprocation, commitment and consistency, social proof, authority, liking, scarcity, and the newest addition—unity (Figure I.1).

At least three of principles can be useful for understanding influencer marketing. First, social proof applies to the way people decide what is

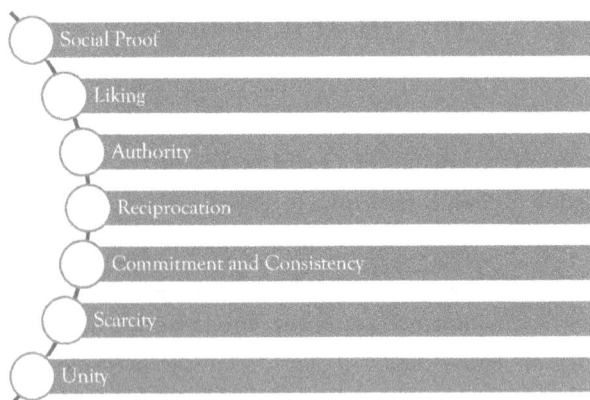

Figure I.1 Principles of persuasion

"correct behavior" by examining how others are performing that behavior and using that evidence as a signal. Influencers are particularly good at presenting brands and other information in a way that gives the impression that "everyone is buying it and so should you." Social proof is particularly important in new situations where people tend to look to others they trust. Generally, social proof is based on experts, celebrities, users, and the wisdom of others that tend to drive influence.[7] Second, liking is very simply that people say yes to the requests of people that are liked. This is explained further in Chapter 4, but the idea of being liked is a very powerful tool for influencers and indeed a foundation of their connection with their audiences. While there are several drivers of liking, for influencers, the issues of attractiveness, similarity, and familiarity are important foundations for credibility. In fact, the power of liking or affinity is often overlooked by marketers who see influence as a matter of reach or popularity exclusively.[8] Last, authority explains the power of people in recognized authority positions (e.g., doctors and specialists). Authority is a powerful tool for influencers who are trying to use their expertise and legitimate experience when promoting a product. Authority can extend to people who are insiders (those with exclusive access), connectors (those who know everyone and have a large network), and activists (those passionate about a cause or issue).[9] Authority is often accompanied by power and title and establishes some type of control. While social influence can be considered the "what" of influencer marketing, and influencers are the "who," exactly how does messages diffuse from brands and influencers out to consumers?

Word of Mouth Marketing

While they are useful for marketers wanting to connect to consumers, influencers can only do so much. The goal of influencer marketing is to get people to act on recommendations. But recommendations need to go beyond one-on-one connections. In general, word of mouth (WOM) is described as informal communications directed at other consumers about particular goods or services which can include product-related discussions and shared content online. It includes direct recommendations and mere mentions.[10] WOM marketing happens when recommendations from an influencer take on a life of its own and travel through a community gaining earned media, whereby people are engaging with and talking about information and recommendations. The efficacy of WOM marketing really depends on why people are talking and listening—including reasons as varied as acquiring information to social bonding to persuading others.[11] WOM marketing is a bit of the Holy Grail for brands. People trust people more than organizations. They trust recommendations from friends and family. These recommendations are incredibly influential. But brands struggle when trying to create the energy around WOM marketing. Brands cannot guarantee that customers will simply mention their products and services on their social media platforms, even if they love the brand. WOM is also tough to scale—getting thousands of people to know about the brand, talk about it, and share it is also truly difficult. So, influencer marketing distributed through social media offers a solution to these challenges around WOM marketing.

Influencer Marketing

The Early Years

The idea of influencers and their connection to marketing has been around for hundreds of years. Some of the earliest influencers include the Pope and a country's royalty—the King and Queen given the expectations from Feudal Law that people would do what they said to do. The Industrial

Revolution ushered in a whole new era of goods that could be purchased which made marketing and advertising important considerations. In the 1800s, British actress Lillie Langtry was linked to multiple brands and Mark Twain endorsed cigars and tobacco products.[12] In the early 1900s, marketers began to tap into the power of celebrities. For example, Murad cigarettes featured Roscoe "Fatty" Arbuckle in print ads making him one of the first celebrity endorsers. Tobacco companies were early adopters of using celebrities in their marketing as both James Stewart and Ronald Reagan endorsed Chesterfields (Figure I.2). Marlboro cigarettes then created the fictional persona of the "Marlboro Man" who set the image for that brand for years. This was one of the first "fictional" endorsers (later joined by everyone from Tony the Tiger for Frosted Flakes to the Jolly Green Giant).[13]

But it was not until the 1980s that the concept of celebrity endorsers really took off. Basketball star Michael Jordan was one of the most popular and influential endorsers, and Pepsi Cola built its brand on using celebrities, including the pop singer Michael Jackson. At the same time, there were early forms of what is now known as influencer marketing. I spoke to Ryan Schram, chief operating officers and president of IZEA,[14] one of the largest influencer marketing firms. The founders of IZEA saw the early potential of the intersection of social media and endorsers for

Figure I.2 Early influencers: celebrities

brands. Schram said that much of influencer marketing had its structural origins in affiliate marketing in the early 1980s. Essentially, affiliate marketing is when a business rewards people or "affiliates" for bringing in new customers. Then, multilevel marketing schemes started to go digital where the original messages were "pass along" e-mail campaigns.

At the same time, versions of social platforms like MySpace allowed users to have a "wall" where they started to create and share content. Most of the content was music—where users copied and pasted clips of music. That was one of the first inklings of the potential of the creator economy. Technology then created live journals, which then became blogs, mostly through the popular Blogger platform (created by Evan Williams and later sold to Google). "Blogger, however, gave people the freedom of starting to combine how to work with a brand and how to create unique content and to start to receive income from that," said Schram. The number of bloggers continued to increase as people found blogging to be a creative outlet for many people and the number of product categories began to expand.

At the time, an early digital pioneer named Ted Murphy was running a digital agency called MindComet (www.mindcomet.com), and as part of the agency offering, Murphy developed proprietary intellectual property that he licensed and sold to clients. One of the early services was the Blog Star Network, which allowed brands access to mommy bloggers. At the time, mommy bloggers (women who blogged about children and lifestyle issues) were one of the largest content creators. Early blogger campaigns were seen as paid advertising—banner ads on blogs. But this started the process of brands paying for access through goods and services in return for bloggers to write about their business. This was also the first way bloggers were able to monetize their work.[15]

But the early days were not easy. There were many problems at first simply because brands tried to tightly control content. Brand managers simply thought of paying bloggers as just another form of paid advertising. "As you might imagine, there were so many misfires and gaffes as that was working itself out because some people saw this as—oh well, I am paying these people, therefore, it should be basically an advertorial and they should do what I say and write exactly what I—the client—want," said Schram.

Remember, at this time, there was no Facebook or Twitter and interestingly, there was a huge backlash about the role of advertising on social media. MindComet was one of the first companies trying to monetize social media (and received a lot of negative push back for it), but Murphy had enough early success to attract venture capital funding in 2005 and 2006 to spin the Blog Star Network into a separate company and rebranded as a company called PayPerPost. "It is credited for being the very first influencer marketing platform, although it was still not called influencer marketing back then and it was openly about paying bloggers to create content for brands," said Schram. "Industry people, even those who people today see as being the forward innovative social thinkers, were saying 'oh no, we should never get paid for working with a brand.' And now that is the entire business model."

Enter Social Media

By the early 2000s, a new type of celebrity—reality stars—became highly influential (and entertaining). Shows such as MTV's Real World was an early innovator that led to top franchises like The Bachelor and The Bachelorette, The Real Housewives, Jersey Shore, and Project Runway among others. Keeping up with the Kardashians, launched the careers of the Kardashians and Jenners, who are now some of the top influencers in the social media age.[16]

Then came the expansion of platforms: Facebook in 2004 and Twitter in 2008. To capitalize on the growth of new platforms, Murphy and MindComet started building out different marketplaces for each of these major platforms (like sponsored tweets for Twitter). Fun fact: PayPerPost (IZEA as it is known now) was the first company using sponsored tweets to pay a little known reality star named Kim Kardashian for a sponsored Tweet.

Murphy then pivoted and rebranded as IZEA which went public in 2011 because larger brands and agencies were doing sponsored social and had increasingly larger budgets. Schram recognized, from his professional background in radio sales, that the most valuable inventory in radio is when an on-air personality (e.g., DJ) opens up to the audience and tells a story about where he went out for dinner. It is not recorded or scripted, but it is effective. "I looked at sponsored social—now influencer market-ing—and I said we are doing all of the mediums and we are democratiz-ing this right because it is going from a broadcast mentality—a one to many—to a many to many medium. It also allows the brand to benefit in a different way. It's not just the implied endorsement … it's not just the reach and awareness and perhaps engagement, which are all important. It is about content creation," said Schram.

By the mid-2010s, the popularity of social media was pivotal to launch-ing social media influencers. Some social media influencers are indeed celebrities and reality stars. Others, however, are normal people who have built their networks and their reputation on social media platforms like Instagram, TikTok, and YouTube. More about them later. Brands and agencies began to figure out how to merge influencer marketing with tra-ditional marketing. According to Addi McCauley, director client strategy and development at IZEA, "Early on there was a heavy public relations (PR) integration. PR people wanted to put out press packages and wanted to get the word out and it was about a very high top of the funnel aware-ness play in terms of where it fit into a plan. Then a lot of PR agencies were starting to move into digital to expand revenue streams so they were able to expand offerings beyond getting clients on *Good Morning America* to being able to help with digital."[17] More pure play digital agencies began to take shape, and then media agencies were also getting into influencer marketing because they viewed influencer marketing as a media play as opposed to a PR initiative. "This has led to influencer marketing being super disjointed across organizations," McCauley added.

Influencer marketing is relatively new (at least in the form that it is currently being used), and there are several definitions of influencer mar-keting, from both academic researchers and marketing practitioners. In Chapter 3, there is a discussion on the foundations for influencer mar-keting definitions from both perspectives. But in order to set the con-text, let's define it. Influencer marketing is the *strategy of compensating people who are influential in specific areas to create and promote content on social media on behalf of an organization or brand with content that captures the attention and trust of the influencer's community, thus opening up new opportunities for the organization or brand.* There are also several misconceptions about influencer marketing. Influencer marketing is not advertising (although oftentimes paid media is used to boost content). Rather influencer marketing is larger than a simple transaction between the brand and the influencer and the influencer and their audience. It is based on relationships. While most of what I cover here is based on social media, influencer marketing can be much broader. Influencers simply use social media platforms to extend their relationship with their audience. Given that, influencer marketing can take place through live events and other initiatives that are not solely online.[18]

The (Current) State of the Industry

In 2021, the industry has grown—not just in the amount of money that brands spend on influencer marketing but in the number of major and minor players in the influencer marketing ecosystem. In fact, by the end of 2019, there were more than 1,100 platforms and influencer marketing focused agencies operating in the market. To give some context, there were 190 such entities in 2015.[19] On each side of the equation are the demand—the brands (large and small)—and the supply—the influencers (well known and not). Social media platforms are the connective tissue— where the influencers build their audiences and where brands build their images. In between there are several intermediaries, which help brands and influencers as well as technology that facilitates campaign development and measurement. Given the nature of the evolution, traditional agencies, media agencies, PR agencies, digital agencies, and of course, influencer marketing agencies are all playing a role depending on the brand's needs. And many of the entities work together. Technology is playing a more important role than in the past. There's not a one size fits all approach. "Each of my clients is its own special snowflake in that they are all different," said Addi McCauley, IZEA.

Let's examine the ecosystem (Figure I.3).

Social Media Platforms

Social media is a technology centric ecosystem where a diverse set of behaviors, interactions, and exchanges involving interconnected actors— individuals, companies, and organizations—can occur. Social media is now pervasive and culturally relevant.[20] The primary social media

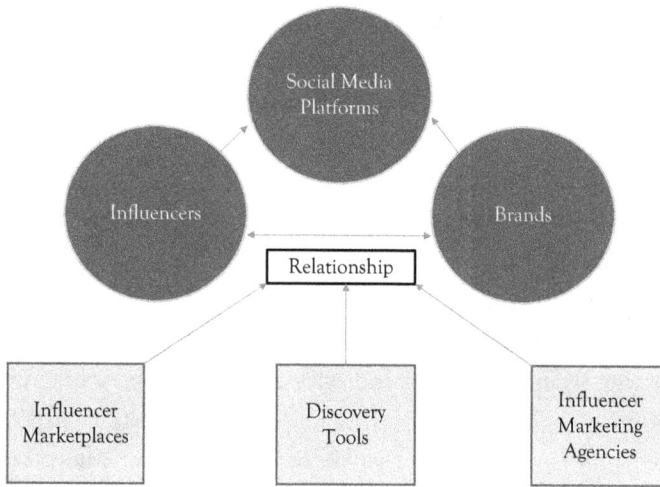

Figure I.3 "Influencer marketing ecosystem"

platforms used for influencer marketing include Instagram, TikTok, and YouTube as the current frontrunners. Pinterest is also making a resurgence given the visual nature of the platform. That said, other social media platforms such as LinkedIn and Facebook also include some influencer marketing campaigns. Clubhouse and Dubsmash are also options. The advantages and disadvantages of the social media platforms are discussed in Chapter 5.

Influencers

Influencers are people who create and disseminate content to audiences that they have built on social media platforms. Influencers include well-known celebrities, reality stars, and a variety of types of influencers. The advantages and disadvantages of influencers are discussed in Chapter 2.

Brands and Organizations

Brands are businesses that sell products and services to consumers and other businesses. Many of these use marketing and advertising as ways to gain awareness and sales. Some brands develop influencer campaigns in house and some use intermediaries. In most cases, influencer marketing falls to either the brand management team or the digital, social media, and web development teams. In a few cases, it falls to the creative development team. Brands use influencers in a variety of ways, and the mechanics of campaign development are discussed in Chapter 5.

There are several intermediaries that assist in connecting influencers and brands, facilitating relationships between influencers and brands and measuring the effectiveness of campaign efforts.[21] It is impossible to develop definitive lines as the industry is undergoing a technological revolution as well as a flurry of acquisitions and mergers. In order to provide tangible examples, I spent some time reviewing IZEA's ecosystem offerings after talking with Ryan Schram and Addi McCauley. First, there are companies that help brands understand the nature of the conversations happening online. *Social media listening tools* are designed to know who is talking about a brand online, what they are saying, where they are saying it, and what they are saying about the competition. Social media listening tools are also used to monitor brand reputation. Examples include companies like Meltwater, Brandwatch, and Mention (among many others). IZEA created Brand Graph, which marketers can use to identify and measure brand share of voice, engagement metric benchmarks, category spending estimates, sentiment analysis, and influencers in the category. Essentially, Brand Graph is a content analysis engine that analyzes and aggregates influencer content (www.izea.com). Second, there are tools that assist brands to *discover influencers*. Many are primarily Instagram centric (for now) and are not based on opt ins from influencers. These allow brands to filter through millions of users to find effective influencers. A few companies include Hypr, Neoreach, and Upfluence (among many others). Some of these also focus on specific platforms like TikTok or Instagram.

Influencer Marketplaces

Influencer marketplaces are newer and involve influencers opting into a marketplace platform to participate. Most offer a range of tools, but generally it is a two-sided platform between influencers and brands. Many influencers participate in multiple platforms. That said, these marketplaces also do some of the tough work around communication between brands and influencers and facilitate payment to influencers. Marketplaces attempt to make the process more seamless for both brands and influencers. Marketplaces also help with influencer discovery, campaign management, reporting, payment, contract negotiation and execution, connection with paid media, campaign tracking, and fake follower detection. The advantages of influencer marketplaces are that they are easy to use since everything is initiated in one place. This also lowers the barriers to entry for smaller brands and influencers since marketplaces assist with some of the more expensive tasks of campaign execution. Some disadvantages depend on the size of the marketplace. If it is too small, this limits the choice to brands. Because influencers opt in, there is little quality control. There can also be issues around time intensity for brands since some of the campaign implementation still falls to the brand's team. There are advantages to influencers as well. "Because we are communicating with our influencers on such a regular basis, the reason that influencers sign up to be part of a network is that we have a lot of deal throughput," said McCauley speaking about IZEA's Unity Suite and Shake platforms. Unity Suite is the core platform that is the legacy marketplace of influencers. Shake is a newer marketplace that gives anyone direct access to hiring creators.

A few marketplaces include IZEA and ExpertVoice. IZEA has IZEAx-Discovery. It is a comprehensive influencer search platform that uses artificial intelligence (AI) and machine learning to provide data for marketers about specific influencers. Some of the data include follower counts, the quantity of sponsored content, engagement rate over time and with specific assets, and content performance. IZEAxDiscovery is used with its influencer marketplace called Shake. Shake provides a seamless way for brands and creators and influencers to work.

DIY Influencer Campaign Tools

Some brands want to design and implement influencer marketing campaigns and just need some help making that happen. Some of the discovery platforms and marketplaces have additional tools that allow this to occur seamlessly. IZEA's Unity Suite allows brands to search for influencers; communicate with them; create content; facilitate bidding, payment, and budgeting; distribute content; and monitor the results. This can be seen as an extension of a brand's in-house capabilities.

Influencer Marketing Agencies

There are agencies that specialize in matching not only brands and influencers but also content production and measurement. VaynerMedia, Obviously, Collectively, Captiv8, and 360i are all good examples of influencer agencies. Other influencer marketing agencies marry supply and demand by providing deep services to influencers and providing full service for brands. The primary reason to work with an agency is that it is full service meaning discovering and matching influencers, contracting, paying influencers, tracking results, and ensuring brand safety and Federal Trade Commission (FTC) disclosure results. The benefits include industry partnership that are well established with influencers, solid experience, access to data (which can be expensive), and campaign management. However, this comes with a price, and depending on the agency, it may be limited to digital marketing only as opposed to cross channel, integrated campaigns.

Estate Five is one such agency out of Dallas (with offices in Beverly Hills and New York) that focuses on mid- to macro-influencers. Estate Five provides a full suite of business services to influencers—from contact negotiation and payment to accounting and legal services. They also review content and ensure compliance with FTC disclosure. Five Estate essentially help them run their businesses. "We provide influencers with the services and experience in a space that is constantly evolving that they would not have on their own just sort of operating in a vacuum," said cofounder and CEO of Estate Five Lynsey Eaton. Additionally, the company works with brands who want to work with their stable of talent and help with all aspects of planning and executing campaigns. Estate Five is also joined by a host of other companies that are essentially talent agencies for influencers. These include the likes of Viral Nation, NeoReach, Central Entertainment, and others.[22]

Other players in the ecosystems such as venture capital firms focus on the creator economy including ways to recognize and monetize the value of top creators as well as startups that help facilitate everything of community building to ecommerce, to customer relationships management and financing for creators. These are changing by the day as capital is poured into the ecosystem. Consider that an up-and-coming social media platform Clubhouse is an audio-only app that is already valued at more than $4 billion. It did not really exist a year ago. There are also niche players in the ecosystem dedicated to serving both brands and influencers. Talent agencies have also added influencers to their roster of clients. Last, there are numerous tools and technologies to assist influencers to create their work.[23] More about this in Chapter 2. There is a lot to learn and a lot to keep up with as the industry grows and matures.

The Roadmap

Take a look online, and there is some fantastic content out there to learn how to be an influencer. Blogs, e-books, webinars, and courses—all great tools to learn about influencer marketing—are at the fingertips. There are also some really great books and podcasts too. I know ... I have read them and listened to them. I particularly liked books by Amanda Russell and Neal Shaffer—both of whom examined influencer marketing—and in particular—social media influencers from a "boots on the ground" perspective. Both are influencers in their own right. Given the great practical content available, I decided to write a slightly different book. While this book is grounded in the practical implications for brands (including interviews with several people actively working in the business), it also incorporates academic research on celebrity endorsers as well as emerging research on social media influencers. There has been increased attention in social media influencers over the past 8 to 10 years, and much more to be learned. The goal for this book is to serve as the bridge between the rapidly increasing technological innovation that brands face when designing a campaign, the growing cultural capital that many social media influencers have, the growth in tools to facilitate the massive interest in the creator economy in general, and the theoretical foundations to help marketing managers to understand the "why" and "how" influencer marketing campaigns can work more effectively.

As part of this effort, I was able to talk with several very influential people working in influencer marketing as well as some people who have been instrumental in getting the work done. A huge thank you to Ryan Schram, COO and President of IZEA; Addi McCauley, Director, Client Development and Strategy at IZEA; Lynsey Eaton, cofounder and CEO Estate Five; Andrea Arias, Associate Brand Manager for Cetaphil (Galderma); Brittany Knight, lifestyle marketer for Nike, Speakers on

Adweek's Social Media Week LA conference held virtually June 29 to July 1, 2021; West Gissinger, Sessions Pilates fitness instructor, fitness influencer and brand ambassador for Outdoor Voices and Carbon38; and Preston Campbell, social media content creator for Kameron Westcott of the Real Housewives of Dallas and founder of Big Mood Marketing.

This introduction sets the roadmap for the rest of the book. The purpose of this introduction is to lay the foundation of social influence and the use of WOM marketing to disseminate brand messages. Theories related to social influence and WOM set up a good foundation to drive the efficacy of influencer marketing. Chapter 1 examines how marketing has shifted in the past with an emphasis on digital marketing, specifically content marketing, native advertising, and influencer marketing. It also introduces the Influencer Marketing Relationship Framework to examine how these concepts work together. Chapter 2 introduces the concept of the creator economy and examines what is driving people to become "creators" and build businesses around it. Chapter 3 defines influencer marketing and social media influencers—no easy task since there are no standard definitions of either concept. This chapter also examines the legacy of celebrity endorsers—traditional celebrities known for something outside of social media—and how they have been used for marketing. Chapter 4 examines the theories that have been used in the celebrity endorsement context. Social media influencers are a specialized case of endorsement, and new research on how social media influencers are similar and different to traditional celebrities is used to set forth a foundation for campaign creation. Chapter 5 examines how to design an effective campaign—everything from setting campaign goals and matching influencers and brands to designing the campaign format and gauging the results. Chapter 6 examines the results of influencer marketing campaigns as well as other issues to consider—from unintended consequences to FTC disclosure requirements. The last chapter examines the future of influencer marketing. The book balances practitioner content with academic research, with interviews sprinkled in so that the reader can get a full view of everything influencer marketing.

CHAPTER 1

The Influencer Marketing Relationship Framework

NFL Engages Generation Z

The powerhouse brand, the National Football League (NFL), is a mature brand but a dominate brand. However, about three years ago, the organization noticed that it was beginning to see a slow loss of young fans. "The brand began to feel a bit stale and overly conservative. I like to look at brands like people and the NFL was starting to seem like a cranky old man," said Tim Ellis, executive vice president and chief marketing officer in a session during AdWeek's Social Media Week LA in June 2021. "We needed to manage it now or we would regret it later." So, they begin a targeted effort to connect with the youth segment and embrace youth culture and a huge piece of this was engaging with the players outside of football. This made sense since this is who the players are. The NFL's strategy was based on connecting passion points for Generation Z, including fashion, music, wellness, and gaming. This was particularly important in 2020 as the NFL was looking to connect to fans and create a new experience since there would be no fans at games. The NFL did this using an influencer relationship marketing framework (discussed as follows) that included elements of content marketing, native advertising, and influencer marketing. For content, they focused on several things but one of the most visible was the Showtime Cam. Since there were no fans in the stadium, the game environment lacked energy. In collaboration with Bud Light, the Showtime Cams were installed in stadiums so that fans and players could celebrate touchdowns together. On Twitter, NFL fans can tag their tweets with #ShowtimeCam and #BudLightSweepstakes to participate in the Showtime Cam during a regular season game. This allowed both Bud Light and the NFL teams to partner to engage fans in different ways given the pandemic constraints. The NFL was also able to use the content across all social media platforms. In order to celebrate the ProBowl, the NFL partnered with Verzuz, which is an online series by Swizz Beatz and Timbaland, that pitted players on their 10 best on field highlights (even going back to high school and Pop Warner days). This was a great way to increase the excitement around the ProBowl and really highlight the players. In terms of influencers, the TikTok tailgate was a collaboration with TikTok and Miley Cyrus for a Superbowl pregame show held for health care heroes. Cyrus ended up posted about the event as well as other guests at the event. The NFL supports players by providing content and media support with everything from gaming to fashion, including supporting product collaborations. The NFL also supported players and causes such as Carl Nassib and the Trevor Project to support LGBTG+ teens and ways to remember and support victims of social justice all of which are important to players and younger fans. NFL, in this case, reached out to new influencers, used new platforms, and other platforms in new ways and found better ways to support the creative efforts of its players. As such, it found new ways to connect with Generation Z.[1]

How Has Marketing Changed?

Marketing has changed dramatically. And it continues to change as the pace of technology increases and audiences continue to adapt their media habits and consumption patterns. For years, marketing and advertising were dominated by personal sales forces, television advertising, newspaper and magazine advertising, and direct mail. Audiences were considered primarily from demographic perspectives. Descriptions like women 18 to 24 with a household income of $40,000 would dictate the marketing mix. Most people got their news from the evening new shows or from the many newspapers that existed in large cities and small communities.

Over the past several years, marketers have shifted marketing budgets from traditional advertising (such as television ads and newspaper ads) to digital advertising (such as search and display ads). In 2020, marketers spent $121 billion on digital advertising in the United States, representing 54 percent of total advertising spent. This is expected to increase to an estimated $153 billion by 2024. The retail industry is the biggest spender in the digital advertising categories. Facebook is the social media platform that gets the most as social media spending represented $37.9 billion in 2020. Programmatic digital display advertising is a use of technology that allows brands to put display ads on publisher websites and represented $63.36 in 2020 with search advertising a close second at $62 billion. Digital video advertising, the placement of ads online based on keywords, represented almost $10 billion in 2020.[2] Indeed, a 2018 CMO Survey reported that social media spending (of all types) represents 13.8 percent of brand's total marketing budget.[3] Overall, marketers have shifted their budget to digital and social media platforms and away from traditional platforms like television and print media.

There are several reasons for this shift in strategy. First, traditional marketing strategies are "push" strategies meaning that the advertising messages are designed and placed to interrupt audiences as they are consuming media such as television shows or newspapers. As consumers have gained more control of their time and media access, push marketing has fallen out of favor relative to pull marketing strategies. The American Marketing Association defines pull marking as a brand's attempt to attract customers via providing valuable content, usually delivered via social media. It is the heart of content marketing, which is described later. Increasingly pull marketing on social media allows for more transparency between consumers and brands, creating a deeper opportunity for relationship building between people and brands. Communication becomes more akin to a conversation since the communication is no longer just one way. Additionally, pull marketing provides a solution to ad blocking technology and the general increase in advertising clutter over the past few years. All are trying to gain attention from consumers, but as consumers gain more control, push marketing is ignored.

Second, more people are using social media in general ($4.14 billion globally)[4] and people are spending a lot of time on social media. While there are many ways to look at social media, Appel and colleagues define social media as "a technology centric—but not entirely technological—ecosystem in which a diverse and complex set of behaviors, interactions, and exchanges involving various kinds of interconnected actors (individuals and firms, organizations and institutions) can occur. Social media is pervasive, widely used and culturally relevant."[5] They further argue that social media has essentially "become almost anything—content, information, behaviors, people, organizations, institutions—that can exist in an interconnected, networked digital environment where interactivity is possible" (p. 80). In the United States, the average adult spends two hours and three minutes on social media each day. Also, note that this probably does not accurately count younger audiences as 13 is the official age for an account. It's estimated that younger audiences spend more than three hours each day on social media, primarily on their mobile devices.[6] While Facebook is still the largest social media platform (with 1.79 billion daily active users), there have been several other options gaining attention. Instagram is the photo- and video-based social platform where the average user spends an average of 27 minutes daily. More than 64 percent of users of Instagram are between 18 and 29, great for engaging Millennials and Generation Z audiences. The average U.S. adult spends, on average, 24 minutes each day with YouTube (the most visited social media website in the United States) and the site is seeing an increase in the time spent by younger audiences.

New (and nearly new) platforms are gaining attention especially from young audiences. Snapchat, once thought to be dead, has made a major comeback with 46 million monthly active users. Users spend an average of 28 minutes daily on Snapchat, and it is one of the most popular social media platforms with Generation Z. Snapchat was also named the most innovative company of 2020 by Fast Company. TikTok is one of the stickiest platforms for younger audiences. TikTok is a video sharing platform specializing in short 15-second videos. More than 32 percent of users are aged 10 to 19 and another almost 30 percent are aged 20 to 29. Users spend an average of 46 minutes on TikTok each day. TikTok was the most downloaded app in 2020 with more than 100 million U.S. users (TikTok is based on China and was merged with Music.ly in 2018).[7] Twitch is a live streaming platform for video games. The average user spends more than 95 minutes daily on the platform, and the platform is particularly popular with younger (and male) audiences.[8]

Third, given the explosion of social media platforms, there are many more opportunities for smaller, more niche products and audiences. The concept of the long tail explains how many products can be sold in small quantities, rather than only relying on the most popular products.[9]

Technology, such as that which powers Amazon, Apple Music, and Spotify, allows people to have access to millions of different products easily and cheaply. This idea has also enabled many people—not just celebrities—to influence the attitudes and behaviors of others. Influencers with small numbers of followers but with higher engagement have been found to be very successful for many brands using influencer marketing.

Fourth, given the ubiquity of digital marketing and, more specifically, the usage of smartphones, brands think about digital and mobile strategies first as opposed to adapting traditional marketing messages to these newer formats. Research shows that people are spending more time on their smartphones or other mobile devices (3 hours and 10 minutes on average in 2019) and are also multitasking more than ever.[10] Taken together with the decline in push marketing, more consumers are searching, buying, and being influenced online. But privacy is also a bigger issue. Users are pushing back on how their data are shared and ad blocking technology is increasing, making it harder to target and retarget advertising to them.

Last, despite (or because of) the lack of trust in organizations and institutions, people trust people.[11] Research from Nielsen says that 92 percent of people are likely to trust a recommendation from a friend.[12] This is much higher than trust levels with brands or companies. And despite U.S. obsession with celebrities in all forms, this trust does not necessarily translate to them. Increasingly, Millennials and Generation Z are turning to influencers and their recommendations. One survey stated that 82 percent said they were likely to follow the recommendation of influencers.[13] All these trends have led to brands pursing a mobile first strategy and the explosion content and social media influencers.

Categorizing Digital Marketing Efforts: Paid, Owned, and Earned Media

From the perspective of a brand, what is content and how (and by who) is it distributed? Brand communications in social media are defined as any "piece of brand-related communication distributed via social media that enables internet users to access, share, engage with, add to and co-create."[14] In an effort to build out integrated marketing communication strategies, many brands have categorized their marketing efforts, especially their digital marketing strategy as paid, owned, or earned media. *Paid media* is purchased advertising space, whether as paid search advertising on Google or sponsored posts on Facebook. This includes pay per click, display advertising, retargeted advertising, paid sponsorships, and paid social media advertising. Brands purchase space to display their message, and it is used to boost social media content. Additionally, traditional media is considered paid media, such as radio, magazine, newspaper, and television advertising, all of which has fallen out of favor. *Owned media* is simply content that is created by the brand and which is then disseminated on brand websites and social media platforms. This includes videos, articles, webinars, and a host of other tactics. This also includes brand-specific web development. Owned media also includes efforts at search engine optimization (SEO) that allows audiences to find quality content without the brand using paid media. *Earned media*, with roots in PR, happens when content is shared and talked about. This includes

Dunkin Donuts Goes Local

How does a legacy brand like Dunkin Donuts get renewed attention among new audiences? Even though everyone loves coffee and donuts, right? Dunkin Donuts wanted to target a young, digitally centric audience. As a major player in the food and beverage industry, the company generated more than $300 million in coffee sales alone. It was starting to take on Starbucks in a meaningful way. So, Dunkin Donuts decided to pursue a "coffee first" strategy by working with nano- and micro-influencers to improve social media engagement. Campaign goals include increasing awareness of a coffee first strategy as part of its rebranding efforts; raise awareness of the handcrafted espresso and capitalize on its popularity and to improve Instagram engagement and gain more followers. The Dunkin marketing team then reached out to influencers with fewer than 50,000 followers in the greater Philadelphia area, with an emphasis on maximizing authenticity for the brand. Results include 1.1 million followers targeted; 21K+ likes and 965 comments; and 5.2 percent engagement rate. Interestingly, nano-influencers created greater engagement.[15] Brands are now approaching their marketing efforts in a very different way.

online and offline mentions, shares, reposts, and retweets of content about the brand (both positive and negative). Much of paid, owned, and earned media is manifested as content marketing, native advertising, and influencer marketing.

That said, these three strategies—content marketing, as the primary way to create valuable information for customers; native advertising, that seeds that content on social media platforms by paying for space; and influencer marketing, which serves as both a content creation tool and an amplification tool to reach targeted audiences—are separate but related. Elements of content marketing and native advertising converge with influencer marketing making it extremely effective at changing consumer behavior, especially for younger audiences. Figure 1.1 shows that convergence.

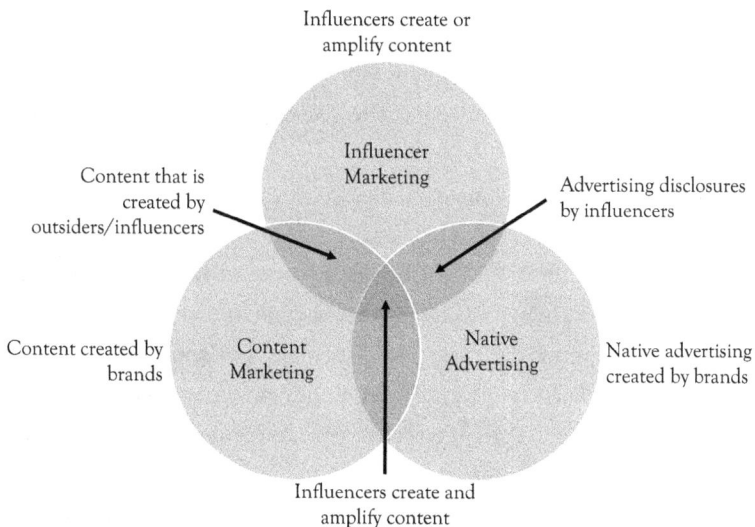

Figure 1.1 Influencer marketing relationship framework

In order to better understand these strategies, let's take a look at each of them in more detail.

Content Marketing

One of the marketing strategies that has gained popularity, especially with the growth of social media, is content marketing (also referred to as owned media). The Content Marketing Institute defines content marketing as "a strategic marketing approach focused on creating and distributing valuable, relevant and consistent content to attract and retain a clearly defined audience within the objective of driving profitable customer action." A majority of brands utilize content marketing in some way to increase sales, save money, and attract more loyal customers. In fact, it is considered the most effective tool in the marketing arsenal.[16] Content marketing is an important part of digital marketing relating to SEO, PR, and paid advertising. It is often used at different points of the purchasing funnel—from general awareness to point of purchase depending on the message and the industry. For example, let's assume a customer is investigating whether or not to purchase a new project management software. Early in the search, the customer may read a blog article comparing several options and then watch a video highlighting the features. This can then lead to signing up for an informational webinar before finalizing the purchase. Each of these—blogs, videos, and webinars—are examples of content that will be more or less effective depending on that purchase funnel interaction.

Research shows that content marketing is gaining ground. According to the Association of National Advertisers (ANA), spending on content marketing has seen a 73 percent budget increase in the past three years. More than 70 percent of marketers invest in content marketing, and while most are maintaining their budget, 24 percent are expecting to increase that investment. Marketers are using content marketing to target multiple audiences, and 40 percent of marketers say that content marketing is very important to their overall marketing strategy.[17] As demand has increased, marketers have outsourced some of their needs to agencies or content creators. They have also built in-house resources. An ANA survey stated that 78 percent of marketers have some sort of in-house agency function, a large increase from the prior five years.[18] One way that brands also obtain content is through user-generated content, which is content that has been collected and created by regular customers and shared on their branded social media. This is proven to be an increasingly effective manner of gaining access to content, especially given its authenticity.

Brands report an 84 percent increase in the amount of content created in the past two years.[19] The primary types of content include videos, e-books, blogs, infographics, photography, case studies, white papers, checklists, trend pieces, interviews, industry highlight features, life and advice articles, topical overview videos, and lists.[20] Content marketing is effective for both business-to-consumer and business-to-business. Videos are the most effective forms of content marketing, specifically promotional videos and brand storytelling videos, and as such, marketers are increasing their investment in video given the higher levels of engagement especially with younger audiences. Most brands are creating content for their own websites as well as Facebook, which continues to be the primary place where content is placed. Content marketing continues to grow, providing more demand for content creators.

Native Advertising

Native advertising is another way that marketers can distribute content, primarily through purchasing ad space.[21] It is described as an "umbrella term that refers to many different ad types, such as those appearing in keyword searches (e.g., Google Ads), on publishers' websites (e.g., *Wall Street Journal*) and social media platforms and feeds (e.g., Facebook)."[22] Native advertising is sponsored content describing any paid advertising that takes the specific form and appearance of editorial content from the publisher itself.[23] To many, native advertising is in the eyes of the beholder. Native advertising is typically high-quality, useful content that is highly targeted and is largely found on social media platforms (e.g., Facebook, Instagram, and LinkedIn) and brands pay for the placement of content on these platforms via several native ad formats. However, because native ads are similar to the format of the platform, it does not necessarily look like advertising. It should be noted that the amount spent on paid social is estimated to be $58.66 billion in 2021.[24]

Brand spending on native advertising is estimated to be $52.75 billion in 2020, and research shows that it is more effective than traditional digital advertising such as display advertising. This spend represents a 20 percent growth in the past four years. Native advertising is moving to be more hyper-targeted, and retargeting will continue to be effective in conversion.[25]

There are various content forms of native advertising including videos, images, infographics, and articles. The audience experience remains intact because native ads are delivered in a way that intentionally looks like other content on the platform. The Internet Advertising Bureau (IAB) set forth six key issues to consider when determining categorization of native advertising (regardless of where they are placed). They include the following:[26]

- Form: How does the ad fit within the overall page design? It is in the viewer's activity stream or not in stream?
- Function: Does the ad function like the other elements on the page in which it is placed? Does it deliver the same type of content experience (e.g., a video on a video page) or is it different?
- Integration: How well do the ad unit's behaviors match those of the surrounding content? Are they the same (e.g., linking to an on-site story page) or are new ones introduced?
- Buying and targeting: Is the ad placement guaranteed on a specific page, section, or site or will it be delivered across a network of sites? What type of targeting is available?
- Measurement: What metrics are typically used to judge success? Are marketers more likely to use top-of-the-funnel brand engagement metrics (e.g., views, likes, shares, time spent) or bottom funnel ones (e.g., sales, download, data capture, and register)?
- Disclosure: Is the disclosure clear and prominent?

Research does that 77 percent of people did not realize that native content was advertising making the issue of disclosure particularly important.[27] Disclosure language and placement includes language such as "sponsored content" that shows up alongside the native ad or #ad. Sometimes sponsored content is created by a third-party content producer (who can be influencers in the industry) and is usually a sponsored video and/or a social media post. Other disclosure language options include "presented by," "featured partner," or "suggested post." The IAB also outlined several advertising options including the following:

- In-Feed Ad units: Ads located within the website or social media platform's normal content feed.
- Paid Search ads: Ads appearing in the list of search results generally found above or below the organic search results. This is typically found when searching in Google or any search engine and are based on keywords in the search matching up to keywords in the ad.
- Recommendation widgets: Ads that are part of the content of the social media platform delivered through a widget that includes "you might like" or "recommended for you."
- Promoted listing: Ads that are usually featured on websites that are not content based and are presented identically to other products on the website.
- In-Ad: This is an ad that fits in a standard IAB unit found outside of the content feed.
- Other: These are typically custom or other formats that are not categorized otherwise.

Generally, consumers fail to recognize and understand native ads as paid content, which leads them to respond more favorably to these new formats than other forms.[28] As such, the FTC has made native advertising an enforcement priority. There will be more information on disclosure and regulation in Chapter 6.

Essentially brands have developed content in various forms of content and then seed them on social media platforms by paying for native advertising. However, many brands struggle with this. No matter how hard they try, they still approach it from an advertising lens as opposed to engaging authentically with customers. Despite all of the conferences and trainings, brands are unable to create content that is compelling as influencers and are unable to reach unique audiences in the same way that influencers can. Most customers are not interested in a relationship with a brand.[29] They are more interested in relationships with people, and social media happens to be the domain for those relationships. And influencer expert Neal Schaffer states that brands should shift their investment of time and money from paid ads and paid social to "joining the conversation with customers who have some influence on social media … people rule social media and always will."[30] Which leads to the third element—influencer marketing.

Influencer Marketing

Influencer marketing builds upon the age-old model of using celebrity endorsers to increase brand awareness and product purchases. However, influencer msarketing doesn't only depend on celebrities. Rather, the more effective strategy is leveraging people who have amassed an audience on social media platforms as key brand advocates. In a nutshell, an influencer is someone who posts to social media in exchange for compensation. Sometimes the influencer is a celebrity known for something (e.g., actor and musician) or s/he can be someone who has built a large following on social media platforms like YouTube, Instagram, TikTok, and Twitch, usually in a specific area of interest or industry (e.g., gaming, fitness, beauty, and cooking). Influencer marketing is the fastest growing part of the marketing mix with brands spending $10 billion in 2020,[31] and eMarketer estimates that influencer spending (only the payments to influencers—not free products or paid media) will grow more than 30 percent in 2021 to $3 billion and more than $4 billion in 2022.[32] Research shows that 75 percent of advertisers reported using influencers in their marketing strategies and 43 percent expect to increase spending.[33] Most brands reportedly have a dedicated influencer marketing budget, and 91 percent believe influencer marketing is an effective strategy. To meet these needs, the influencer marketing industry has exploded with more than 1,120 influencer marketing focused platforms and agencies, with 380 of them created within the past year.[34]

Additionally, influencer marketing seems to garner higher levels of trust with consumers than other strategies. An Edelman study indicated that 63 percent of consumers trust what influencers say about brands, even more than the brands. Influencer-produced branded content is more organic, authentic, and direct to potential consumers than brand-generated ads. In fact, brands don't necessarily need celebrities, despite some high-profile examples like Kylie Jenner and The Rock. One survey showed that consumers are more likely to purchase based on a recommendation from a noncelebrity than a celebrity which has led to the increase in the use of so-called micro-influencers who are people with smaller followings but high engagement audiences.[35] An ANA survey found that more brands are using midlevel and micro-influencers and fewer are using macro-influencers with large audiences.[36]

Interestingly, there are several factors that have increased the importance of influencer marketing. First, the global pandemic and trends in youth consumption habits have increased their influence with their younger audiences.[37] One study showed that influencers are as "influential as ever" especially with 13- to 18-year olds.[38] Generation Z admits to following more influencers than celebrities and also are more making purchases based on this advice.[39] Additionally, influencers have been at home over the past year and have been able to spend more time on content creation, and Generation Z is spending more time at home and online and less with people in person due to the pandemic. Second, social media traffic increased over the past year—Instagram and Facebook by 40 percent—for those under 35 years old, and people are viewing a variety of content types and topics (e.g., meditation, fitness, cooking, and self-help). Last, influencers have been increasingly effective at creating content that is valuable to their audiences, and as such, they are able to deliver targeted messages to hard-to-reach audiences.[40] This is resulting in high engagement rates and is especially the case for influencers with small numbers of followers (called micro-influencers and nano-influencers).

This comes on the heels of several reports that earlier questioned the efficacy of influencer marketing. The ANA conducted a major study in 2018 that found that while 75 percent of companies engaged with influencers, only 35 percent were convinced it was effective.[41] Brands were concerned about influencers having fake followers as well as the dilution effects of influencers who sponsor too many brands. Additionally, there are continuing issues around disclosure.[42] However, some of the concerns have dissipated in the past year given the return on investment (ROI) and attention that influencer marketing has garnered.

While influencer marketing is important, it rarely works in a vacuum. Let's take a look at an iconic new brand that has revolutionized a product category.

Blue Apron Is Cooking for Real People

Blue Apron is an ingredient and recipe meal kit service that delivers fresh ingredients to homes across the county. While it was an innovator in the meal prep category, it is also in a very competitive landscape. In order to gain awareness, Blue Apron used the influencer marketing relationship framework but using content marketing, influencer marketing, and native advertising. While it would make sense to partner with chefs and foodies, Blue Apron instead matched their influencers with the personas of their customers. The idea was to promote that a home-cooked meal is accessible to everyone! First, Blue Apron identified its customers' pain points. The overall pain point for everyone was that it was tough to prepare a healthy meal at home quickly. Blue Apron's customer is overwhelmingly female (83 percent), is approximately 29 years old, and lives in the city. Second, Blue Apron selected three audiences to focus on and then matched an influencer to that persona. They used coupon codes to track effectiveness. Influencer created content (content marketing) and posted to their audiences (influencer marketing), and Blue Apron amplified it via paid social media (native advertising).

Audience	Influencer
Entrepreneurs: Running a business takes time and energy and that means there is not a lot of extra time and energy to prepare meals and eat healthy. Blue Apron helps entrepreneurs plan meals that fit into their schedules because they don't have to shop for ingredients.	@missmustardseed (Maureen) An entrepreneur known for her to enthusiasm for interior design and home painting who created Mustard Seed Milk Paint, which is an all-natural nontoxic paint formula for home and furniture. Her personality exemplified how nice it is to have a home-cooked meal.
Parents: Cooking with kids is tough. Choosing something that everyone likes and then having enough for everyone becomes a thankless task. Blue Apron helps parents by having a great selection of options that are pleasing to any palette.	@beautifuldrea (Drea Evans) is a mommy influencers in North Carolina who shares content about being a mom. She has several collaborations with larger brands—all of which appeal to young moms. She promoted Blue Apron's dessert menu.
Diabetics: Living with diabetes comes with a ton of restrictions that nondiabetics don't really understand. Blue Apron partnered with the American Diabetes Association to create a friendly menu.	@tidchick (Jillian Rippoline) is an influencer living with Type I diabetes. She shares her experience and quick tips and has partnered with brands like Starbucks. She promoted the new diabetic friendly menu.[43]

It is evident that influencer marketing will be an important addition for some brands (and potentially a main driver for others). However, there is much to be learned about influencers—these creators who in some cases have built business (and even empires) from cultivating an audience of followers, creating content that resonates with this audience, and partnering with brands that add value to their audience. The next chapter dives into the creator economy and I will provide a brief glimpse of who they and where influencer marketing fits into the larger Creator Economy.

CHAPTER 2

The Creator Economy

Welcome to the Future

The Creator Economy. It is so varied. As such, it is impossible to start the chapter with only one story. So, let's look at three: the creator as content developer, the creator as influencer, and the creator as entrepreneur. One of the best examples of a creator who creates content is a photographer. Think about all of the travel photographers who travel the world, take gorgeous photos, and then either sell the photos using Instagram as a marketing platform or create a large audience and become a magnet for brands. Travis Burke (@travisburkephotograpy) out of California focuses on the natural landscape of national parks. Others like @bemytravelmuse have left the corporate life to lead a more creative life.

The creator as influencer can be anyone, and we learn in this book, you don't have to be a celebrity to do so. West Gissinger @westgissinger on Instagram is an example of successful nano-influencers. West is a Pilates and cycle instructor in Dallas, Texas, and created a popular ab routine that she highlights through videos on Instagram. She posts for Sessions Pilates, as well as serves as a brand ambassador for Outdoor Voices and Carbon38. She also is on Liketoknow.it and a part of an Amazon affiliate program where she has access to affiliate links to a database of brands to tag. "My goal as a content creator and influencer is to show up authentically to encourage, motivate and educate everyday people in the fitness space," said Gissinger. "It is a way for me to build community around my profession. I use social media as a dynamic and real-time business card. It is a way for me to connect to current clients and potential clients. I use it as both a fun and creative outlet, as well as a strategic marketing tool," she added.[1]

The last is the creator as entrepreneur. The beauty brand Glossier launched in 2014 is one of the successful direct-to-consumer (DTC) brands that have deftly used social media and ecommerce as the cornerstone of their value proposition. Valued at $1.2 billion as of 2020, Glossier's beginning was a blog in 2011, written by founder Emily Weiss, who was then an intern at Teen Vogue. The blog called "Into the Gloss" was where Weiss noticed that the beauty industry had an image problem. She wrote articles on beauty issues that were widely popular and that were then augmented with Instagram (early on with 186,000 followers for Glossier—now with more than a million). The beauty industry was failing to portray real women with normal shapes, sizes, and skin. So, she created a company, got funding ($2 million from Kristen Green of Forerunner), and launched with four products. "She was really thinking differently," said Green in an article. "I thought—I need to work with this woman. I don't know what we are going to build, but it's going to be different and interesting," she said.

The tagline "Skin first. Makeup second. Smile always." remains the ethos of the company. The product lines are sparse relative to larger beauty brands. But the insight into what women wanted and needed (and what was not there) paired with the explosion of ecommerce which allowed brands to completely control their own retail experience from product discovery to online experience design to social media initiatives helped launch Glossier.

The company has a relentless obsession with its consumers. Glossier spends a lot of time listening and building its community to the point where customers feel they have a stake in the company. The conversations with consumers exist largely online but within a multichannel conversation. This had led to a cult following and is much more than the result of good market research. Given its roots as a blog, content marketing is the foundation for Glossier's strategy. In addition to the blog, they popularized the "Get Ready With Me" format on YouTube to share beauty routines. The brand's Instagram is their central social media channel, but most of the content is user created and shared, thus making all of its customers potential influencers. All of this attention to people have created a strong community—one that rivals other DTC companies such as Dollar Shave Club, Peloton, Harry's, and Honest Company. Weiss has become a sought-after speaker and leader, as well as one of the few unicorn startups of the past few years.[2]

Who becomes a social media influencer? The rise of the social media influencer—and relatedly, influencer marketing—is the result of a larger trend—the creation and expansion of the Creator Economy. The Creator Economy is the larger ecosystem. Influencers are one part of it (albeit a very visible and fast-growing part of it). Let's start by digging into the Creator Economy and how it differs from earlier models.

Creator Economy

The Creator Economy (also called the Passion Economy) is the fast-growing class of businesses centered around independent content creators, content curators, and community builders. According to a recent *Forbes* article, the creator economy is made up of online platforms, marketplaces, and tools that help democratize and monetize creative expression from anyone.[3] These creators include social media influencers, web content creators, bloggers, podcasters, videographers, and all of the software and finance tools to facilitate that growth and monetization.[4] The Creator Economy has done much to democratize the ways that content is created and produced, distributed, and amplified and consumed by others. Previously, content was dictated by major players—advertising agencies, television and movie producers and studios, music producers and record labels, and publishers of all kinds. Now, creators have more power and audiences have more choice.[5] "Creativity is at its peak in the 2020s, and platforms that support independent creative expressions are springing up more than ever," said technology writer TK Princewall.[6]

Much of the growth of the Creator Economy comes at the expense of the old "Attention Economy"—the advertising-based revenue model that has dominated advertising and creative industries for the past several decades. In fact, some of the largest and most valuable companies—especially in technology—have built their success on this model. Google and Facebook are essentially advertising-based companies. Overall, there has been a major shift from a tangible-based economy (e.g., physical products) to an information-based economy. Attention has become more scarce and more valuable, and several products were "free" in exchange for that attention as well as the personal information that tech companies then sold to advertisers.[7] Eventually, the notion of "free" led to broken trust, misinformation, privacy scandals, and information hacks. Additionally, at the beginning of the Attention Economy, the platforms provided a mass audience important for creators. But soon the leverage of creators increased, barriers to entry for creators decreased resulting in a power shift—away from the platforms and toward creators.[8] Engagement between creators (and influencers) and audiences became the most important currency. So, platforms are now attempting to provide ways for creators to monetize their work. According to Clara Bergendorff, a *Forbes* contributor for venture capital, "It seems the future of digital capitalism is in the hands of many micro-entrepreneurs who are closer, more connected, and by virtue of being niche understand their patrons better than the big brands—whether selling content, products or knowledge."[9] This has major implications. "The creator economy has clearly taken over the world of influence and culture and the rise of creator economy tools have allowed new creators to emerge daily, and existing creators to reach audiences in new ways," said Andrew Omori, Partner at venture capital powerhouse Andreessen Horowitz.[10]

In addition to the major shift from Attention Economy, there are several recent trends that led to growth of the Creator Economy. First, the 2008 recession (and later the 2020 global pandemic) affected full-time job creation and many people found themselves out of work. Second, there has been a social shift where people want to do something they are passionate about as their primary job, want more control over their lives, and want to be their own boss. The economic conditions of the rise of the Gig economy and the ramifications of the global pandemic led to a greater number of content creators with time to pursue their passion. Indeed, there seems to be a rise of "micro-entrepreneurs" who are using digital platforms to make a living by leveraging their skills in the absence of a traditional employer relationship.[11] Third, technology has ushered in the ability to do more at cheaper prices. This includes faster mobile networks (5G), better quality phones and video recorders, larger screens, more apps, and simply more curiosity from creators. Fourth, marketing strategies and media consumption have undergone dramatic changes. Media choice has exploded, technology is ubiquitous, and marketers collect more data on their audiences than ever before making it easier and more effective to target advertiser messages. However, this increasing choice also leads to lower engagement and less attention from audiences, as many install advertising blockers to ignore overt advertising messages.[12] In fact, ad blockers have become a major pain point for traditional digital advertising. All of this has led to the creation of an entirely new content ecosystem, where social media influencers are only part of the story.

These changes and resulting attention led to the major financial impact of the Creator Economy. The Creator Economy spurred more than $800 million in industry growth from only 31 startups since October 2020. April 2021 had the highest capital infusion of $338.8 million, signaling that the Creator Economy is a major player in entrepreneurship and business. The influencer marketing market alone is on pace to exceed $13.8 billion in 2021 while the total Creator Economy is estimated at $104.2 billion. The Creator Economy intersects with the mega "Gig Economy," which is forecasted to reach $455 billion by 2023, with 64 percent of full-time workers saying they want to do side hustles. The Gig Economy, while large, is also known more as a commodity and is prevalent in industries such as food delivery (DoorDash) and transportation (Uber, Lyft). That said, the 14 percent of gig workers are in creative industries.[13]

Who Are the Creators?

According to estimates, more than 50 million people globally consider themselves to be a creator. Most are amateur creators, while more than two million are considered professionals. That will likely grow given the low barriers of entry. A creator is an individual who has created an audience on a digital or social platform and who curates or produces content to meet the needs of that audience.[14] The Creator Economy belongs to everyone who can create—artists, writers, musicians, journalists, dancers, photographers, designers, and video gamers—anyone looking at creative expression. In the past decade, there has been a surge in the Creator Economy, where people who are creating and distributing content for brands are earning income from their efforts. Using social media platforms such as YouTube, Instagram, Snapchat, Twitch, TikTok, and Substack, content creators and entrepreneurs can earn money through a variety of models.

There are at least two important caveats when it comes to monetizing for creators. First, the audience must be built first. Second, once the audience is built, it is important to understand that all audience members are not created equally in terms of their willingness to spend money. Peter Wang in *Creator Economy*[15] argues that there are three types of fans. Casual fans are not willing to pay for much but will likely make up most audience members. Active fans are willing to pay a small amount, while super fans are willing to pay a lot. In fact, venture capitalist Li Jin[16] states that a creator only needs between 100 and 1,000 super fans to earn a strong living. That said, to maximize earnings, it is critical to have multiple income streams targeted at different audiences.

Advertising is aimed at the casual fan, allowing the creator to earn income from the most fans for the lowest price. Subscriptions are recurring income from fans through either paywalled content or community or unlocking some additional value, like community badges. Many creators create tiered subscriptions. Both ads and subscriptions are reliable and are valuable for creators with large audiences (e.g., more than 100,000). Tipping is another option for monetization but is not a reliable source given its variability. Selling digital goods such as eBooks, PDFs, and online courses are great once the audience is built and the creator is delivering consistent value. Digital goods are usually targeted at the super fans. Nonfungible tokens (NFTs) are a newer way for creators to sell unique content to fans. Right now, NFTs are high because they are new and unique and use an auction format.[17] Other ways to monetize include sponsored content, product placement, and brand sponsorship, especially for influencers. There is also affiliate marketing, VIP meetups and fan clubs, and even cocollaboration product launches.

The top content creators make millions. YouTube creator David Dobrik's monthly Adsense checks averaged $275,000 per month for an average of 60 million monthly views. Charli D'Amelio is a 16-year-old TikTok influencer who surpassed 100 million followers making more than $4 million in the past year and a half.[18] The highest paid writers on Substack are earning more than $500,000 annually. The video gamer Ninja earns more than $500,000 a month on Twitch. Even an eight-year-old who reviews toys made $26 million on YouTube. That said, the real riches are only available to those at the top. For example, only the top 3 percent of YouTube creators make more than $17,000 annually in advertising revenue and that requires 1.4 million views per month.[19] These more niche "long tail" communities represent value and are currently underserved and underpaid, even though their fans are incredibility invested and engaged in their work. This continues to be an issue—currently, the Creator Economy has no "middle class."

Instagram Rich Celebrities and Influencers

Social media planning and analytics company Hopper created the Instagram Rich List. Interestingly, numbers 1 through 39 are traditional celebrities—actors, musicians, and athletes. But the rest influencers are social media influencers. Check out a sampling of both top celebrities and then some of the top influencers as of 2020. For a full list, see www.hopperhq.com/blog/2020-instagram-rich-list/

Name	Industry/sector	Instagram followers	Earnings per post
Dwayne "The Rock" Johnson (No. 1)	Celebrity	190 million	$1,050,000
Kylie Jenner (No. 2)	Celebrity	186 million	$986,000
Christiano Ronaldo (No. 3)	Sports	231 million	$889,000
Kim Kardashian (No. 4)	Celebrity	180 million	$858,000
Eleonara "Lele" Pons (No. 39)	Influencer/lifestyle	39 million	$144,000
Huda Kattan (No. 46)	Influencer/beauty	41 million	$91,300
Sommer Ray (No. 48)	Influencer/fitness	24 million	$86,600
Zach King (No. 50)	Influencer via YouTube	23.4 million	$81,100
Charli D'Amelio (No. 56)	Influencer via TikTok	20.6 million	$71,600
David Dobrik (No. 57)	Influencer via YouTube	13.1 million	$69,400

In a survey from NeoReach and Influencer Marketing Hub, the companies explored the earnings of creators (and in particular influencers). What they found was that the traditional idea of influencers making their money from sponsored posts and brand deals is only part of the story. They found that 43 percent make a livable wage from their content (about $50,000 annually). It does take time—46 percent of these creators who are making money have been at it for more than four years.[20] Creators state that they are most concerned about engagement rates over the number of followers. The human connection with their audience seems to be very important to them. In fact, in four out of seven social media platforms, creators listed engagement rate as the top measure of success (platforms included Instagram, TikTok, YouTube, Facebook, Twitch, and Twitter). Instagram is still the most important platform with TikTok taking a surprising second given its age.[21] In IZEA's *2018 State of the Creator Economy* report, they found that most of the creators they surveyed made their money from influencer marketing content with display ads coming in second. They felt that fit with content, audience relevance, compensation, ability to screen, process ease, and timing fits were all important factors when working with a brand.[22]

IZEA conducted a survey of its influencers called the *2021 State of Influencer Equality* report.[23] This report is based on a survey of its marketplace. They found that for the first time, African American influencers earned the most per post in 2020. Smaller populations of non-White influencers paired with marketer demand for diverse voices has driven the price per post up for Hispanic, Asian, and non-White other influencers as well. They also found that sponsorship deals for racial minorities now mimic the general population. Thirty-five percent of the U.S. population is non-White. But 37 percent of the deals went to non-White influencers, showing that brands are increasingly interested in more diverse voices. They also found those who speak Asian languages command a premium as well. Males earn more than female influencers on a per post basis, but the gap is closing. The gap was 24 percent in 2020 down from 47 percent in 2019. But female influencers get a large majority of the deals—90 percent—due to the abundance of brand friendly female influencers. Last, influencers under age 17 command the highest premium for sponsorships. They found that as influencers age, the cost per post declines until age 55 and then bounces back.

The Tools of Creator Economy

According to Influencer Marketing Hub, there are several types of creators: web content creators, YouTube creators, podcast creators, and social media creators. These cover a range of platforms and channels. Web content creators are generally developing blogs, checklists, white papers, eBooks, and case studies. These are common forms of content marketing and utilize both writing and graphic design skills. Some creators are generalists; some are specialists.[24]

YouTube creators typically develop a channel on that platform and build an audience of subscribers. They create and publish videos—some longer form than other platforms—on YouTube. Most YouTubers are "on camera" and do most of the production (editing, writing, and recording) themselves, unless they have a large channel. This is not always easy—YouTube has more than two billion monthly active visitors and 50 million of them are actively creating content, making for a very crowded marketplace. Indeed, 85 percent of YouTube views are generated by only three percent of YouTube channels. But the audience is there—especially among Generation Z, who are more likely to watch YouTube than television.[25]

Podcast creators, such as YouTube creators, develop a podcast "show" with several seasons (perhaps) and episodes. They may do part of the podcast or all of it—from interviewing, writing, recording, editing, and producing. Podcasting has seen a huge surge; as of March 2021, there are more than two million podcasts with more than 47 million episodes. Of those two million, about 750,000 remain active and subscriber numbers increased during the pandemic.[26]

Social media creators, such as web content creators, are writing and creating articles, blogs, guides, e-books, and so forth, but for a specific social media platform. Additionally, their content can include images, testimonials, infographics, contents, and holiday content. Many of the social media creators are also social media influencers since they are often creating this content for a specific audience often useful for brands.[27]

In addition, there are several other types of creators—from networkers who create videos and community events to artists who make how to videos, to teachers who publish tutorials online, and to others. Many of these are not necessarily connected to being an influencer, but rather more of a content creator or marketer. According to *Fast Company*,[28] some of the hottest creator categories include podcasters, writers, video course creators, teachers, personal shoppers, fitness instructors, and virtual coaches.

Want to Be a Creator? What Does It Really Take?

First being a creator is hard work! According to Peter Wang, there are three main steps to becoming a creator. First, the creator needs to publish. To do this, it is important to find a niche and publish frequently (at a minimum once a week, and possibly up to daily). A niche needs to be the intersection of what interests you, what you are good at, and what people want to hear. Even though it may seem counterintuitive, developing a niche—even a niche in a niche—is a key to success. This takes a lot of motivation because to build an audience takes a long time. Second, the creator needs to grow the audience. To do this, learn what content is working and not working with the audience. Be sure to engage and interact with audience members—through responding to comments and even collaborating with other creators. Finally, it is time to make some money. Start by finding ways to monetize the content which ideally will lead to a business. One major consideration is to move the community from a social media platform to an "owned community." Platforms can change policies that may hurt your community so moving to owned helps the creator gain more control.[29]

The Role of Technology

One of the main reasons that the Creator Economy is even possible is the explosion of new technology in the space. Tech is playing a huge role in creative expression, and new tools and platforms spring up daily to help creators pursue their passion of creating. Social media platforms are moving away from an ad-based revenue model to a content-based model. This is good news because the ad-based model does not offer much value to content creators. Instead, some of these same social media platforms are empowering creators with new tools enabling them to become micro-entrepreneurs.

In terms of investments, there are four categories: platforms, tools, monetization enablers, and creator-led businesses. Some combine aspects of each. Social platforms are allowing creators to showcase their work and enable new forms of entertainment. They typically try to solve a utility need with new tools in a new category and then allow for platform stars to develop content. Instagram, TikTok, Substack, and Medium—all of these—are good examples. Platforms like YouTube and Patreon have traditionally supported creators through revenue sharing. Others like Gumroad and Etsy have created marketplaces for creators to sell their products. Breakr is a music marketing platform that bridges the gap between content creators and music labels.[30]

Tools are the next category that assist creators to do their job. This can include ways to improve their work and to facilitate communication among several parties (e.g., between a social media influencer and a brand wanting to employ them for a campaign like an influencer marketplace). Or tools are used as ways to make creator jobs easier. For example, Red Bubble allows for print on demand services allowing for an efficient "production" for some creators.[31]

Technology has also allowed new pays to monetize. Using technology such as cryptocurrency and blockchain, some companies have created efficient ways to connect creators to those who will pay them. Only fans allow creators to receive funding directly from fans on a monthly basis as well as one-time tips and pay per view. Shopify is an e-commerce platform that allows the setup of online stores. NFTs are digital certificates of ownership (of say—memes) on the blockchain which allows creators to authentically own and sell their craft.[32]

Finally, there are the creator businesses—a small subset of all the 50 million creators but who are driven to leverage platforms and infrastructure to become the entrepreneurs of the future.

Connections With Everyday Audiences

But is the audience there? The answer is yes. Several factors have led to more attention aimed at creators. First, 81 percent have U.S. adults have a smartphone[33] and spend more than two hours daily on social media. Indeed, this is particularly the case for younger audiences. Generation Z spend three hours daily on social media platforms and millennials spend two hours 39 minutes on social media platforms.[34] Second, content sharing platforms have increased, including sector agnostic (e.g., Instagram) as well as category-specific platforms (e.g., Twitch). Top platforms for creators include YouTube, Instagram, Twitch, and others aimed at music, podcasts, writers, and illustrators. Some of these new platforms also include different monetization models, such as subscriptions, or in the case of YouTube, creators are paid a small portion of earned ad revenue.[35] Additionally, new platforms are simply fun ways to amass followings without a specific skill (e.g., TikTok). Other platforms for content creators include Amazon publishing, Etsy, Ebay, Twitch, Instagram, YouTube, and others.[36] Third, audiences increasingly have more power and don't trust traditional advertising and more likely to pay attention to people they follow on social media. As such, audiences value user-generated content and are interested in a variety of niche areas. They appreciate that content creators can personally engage with them. The creator economy is directly impacted by the growth of influencer marketing.

But why do Generation Z and millennials want to be influencers? There are a variety of reasons. A report from *Morning Consult* stated that for Generation Z, the top reasons were (1) the opportunity to make a difference in the world, (2) the opportunity to share ideas with an audience, and (3) it is fun and interesting work. Millennials' top reasons included (1) flexible hours, (2) money, and (3) and the opportunity to try new products. These show the varying motivations of two specific audience who are primary drivers of the creator economy.[37] It also shows the dynamics of an ever changing workplace and concept of work that will lead to disruptive innovation.

Many content creators start with writing on a blog or creating a video or audio podcast. From there, they can grow their audience by developing compelling content and engaging in an authentic way. Eventually, the most popular and successful creators can monetize their work in a variety of ways. Here is a great example. Alex Snodgrass, author of the *New York Times* winning cookbook *The Defined Dish: Healthy and Wholesome Weeknight Recipes*, started with a food and wellness blog and built from there. As a native of a small town called Celina, Texas, in the Dallas/ Fort Worth area, and with an Italian mother who was a great cook, Alex started cooking and experimenting while in college to avoid eating out. In fact, she was a popular choice with her college friends due to her cooking talent. After graduating and while staying home with a young daughter, she started a blog in 2014 with her sister. Her sister was a personal trainer and provided the fitness advice, while Alex provided the healthy food and cooking information. The "Defined Dish" was born. Alex refocused the blog in 2016 to make it "real job" after doing the Whole30 diet plan to rid herself of gluten and sugar. For Alex, this newfound health perspective was a gamechanger and launched her influencer empire. She creates and shares hundreds of healthy recipes, focusing on real food that everyone loves. To date, she has more than 575,000 Instagram followers, and in 2020, she released her cookbook. Blogging was the platform that really set Alex as a creator on the path to stardom. Her advice? "I would say that consistency is probably the key. There is no way of knowing how to start a blog, and there is no right or wrong way of doing it. It took me about two years to find my own voice and find my rhythm and get to know what people wanted from me and what I was good at sharing. And, so, I think you've just got to get started, be consistent, and it just kind of evolves into your own brand and your own voice with time. Once you get there is when you can really blossom."[38]

It is clear that influencer marketing, content marketing, and native advertising have changed how most brands market their products and services. The value of influencer marketing is particularly important to millennial and Generation Z audiences, given their interest in social media influencers relative to traditional celebrities. Influencer marketing has played a major role in the "creator economy" which will continue to transform popular culture, marketing, and entrepreneurship. So how can brand managers leverage this knowledge to benefit their products and services?

CHAPTER 3

Celebrity Endorsement and Influencer Marketing

An Overview

The Revolution of Rockstar Energy

Energy drinks as an overall category have not changed much. They are associated with males and extreme action sports. As such, the category needed to expand, and Rockstar Energy, a subsidiary of PepsiCo, wanted to be part of that expansion. Rockstar decided to tap into the "hustle" culture. They defined it as "striving headstrong and voraciously toward a goal" and created the Hustle On campaign which launched during the pregame for the 2021 SuperBowl featuring Lil Baby, skateboarder Chris Joslin, and gaming icon and 100 Thieves founder Nadeshot. It also included real people who are hustling to their greatness. The entire effort celebrates the hustle mentality of Rockstar Energy's target audience.

One of the key strategies was to engage a variety of influencers in a variety of ways. Rockstar Energy decided to build its internal team to establish and cultivate its most important relationships with influencers. They wanted to give their brand a "face" and show that they care about the creator. Rockstar Energy does work with agencies but felt that this move was important and has yielded several benefits for the brand. Their strategy includes a tiered approach to influencers where at the top they are establishing connection and cocreating with influencers and expanding audiences and at the lower tiers they are looking at those who they can build relationships with. "It is like a farm system. The top two tiers are the major league, and the other two tiers are the farm system," said Gabe Alonso, head of digital platforms and community at PepsiCo in a talk at Adweek's Social Media Week LA in June. He cited that both tiers are really important to Rockstar Energy.

Alonso also mentioned that it is important not to cling to strategy when it needs to be loosened up. In the Hustle On campaign, he talked about a partnership with Frank Cook that developed a Varsity Jacket for the Hustle Collective, a group of influencers who embody the brand. Many people wanted the jacket, but Alonso said he stubbornly stuck to the original strategy until it was clear that there was a better way. As such, he opened some creative control and that has been instrumental in developing a relationship with 100 Thieves and its leader Nadeshot on Twitch, expanding the gaming world to Rockstar Energy. Last, Rockstar Energy knows that influencers cannot do it alone and ensures that content can be amplified with a media investment. Going forward, Rockstar Energy is expanding its use of micro- and mid-tier influencers to tell their hustle stories backed by a media investment for the best content.[1]

Opinion Leaders and the Evolution of Influencers

In the beginning of the book, I introduced the concept of influence. Opinion leaders are people who exert influence on the attitudes and behavior of others,[2] and the concept of influencers and opinion leaders have garnered extensive research attention, especially as it pertains to why people purchase certain things. The two-step communication model generally says that people are not influenced directly by media, but rather are influenced through intermediaries who act as opinion leaders in specific areas. Opinion leaders have gained their influence through mass media (in the past) and social media (in the present). Social influence is created through the transmission of opinion leaders' attitudes and opinions to their followers, typically resulting in a form of social persuasion. Two broad research streams for opinion leadership include (1) what characteristics do influencers and opinion leaders possess and (2) how to identify who is influential.[3] When examining influencer characteristics, it is important to understand the type of information that opinion leaders (referred to influencers from here) transmit via their communication to their followers and the domain in which their perceived expertise lies that makes them influential. The literature suggests that influencers can be monomorphic (meaning their expertise lies in one specific domain) or polymorphic (meaning their expertise spans multiple domains).[4] For social media influencers (SMIs), domain knowledge can be based on a specific product category (makeup) or industry (fashion). Over time, some influencers may begin with a singular area of expertise and then expand into other areas (some related; some not), thus making these influencers attractive to a larger number of brands. Sometimes, the information is more utilitarian; other times is not. When considering the type of information transmitted via influencer marketing campaigns, opinion leaders and SMIs can serve as endorsers for brands that offer hedonic value by increasing followers' personal attachment with the brand and/or brands that offer more utilitarian value by providing them functional information.[5]

Generally, opinion leaders come from a variety of demographic backgrounds and, at least initially, have some perceived expertise in a specific area. In fact, expertise has been seen as an important antecedent to social influence and opinion leadership. Early research on opinion leaders shows that typically they can garner media attention, likely to be extroverted, seek the acceptance of others, and are especially motivated to enhance their own social status. They are willing to stand out from the crowd and are generally seen as trustworthy.[6] As such, they are powerful marketing tools.

The second broad research category revolves around how to identify opinion leaders and influencers. While there has been extensive debate on how to identify opinion leaders and influencers in many different contexts, research is starting to identify some of the attributes that are important when determining who an influencer is and relatedly and how to select the most effective influencers for marketing campaigns. While some of the practical ways of identifying influences are discussed in the following, the more strategic decisions will be examined in the next chapter.

Using the theoretical framework of opinion leadership and social influence, marketers have long used "famous" external endorsers in their efforts to sell products. This chapter dives into these efforts by first examining the role of celebrity endorsers in marketing for more than 60 years. Researchers have given celebrity endorsement attention providing a broad spectrum of insights. The point is to examine the newer types of endorsers—namely SMIs—along with the ways that practitioners are designing campaigns and the recent academic research in this area. There are areas of overlap between traditional celebrity endorsers and SMIs. However, there are also some areas where SMIs differ. There is still much to be learned. But first, let's understand the importance of celebrities and marketing.

Celebrity Endorsers and Marketing

Companies have used celebrity endorsements as part of advertising and marketing strategies since the late 19th century.[7] Generally, the use of celebrities has proven to be effective at gaining consumer attention and interest as well as garnering positive consumer attitudes and intentions.[8] Generally, celebrities are perceived as credible, attractive, and well liked and have positive effects on brand evaluations. Given their ubiquity, recent research has reviewed the effects of celebrity endorsers.[9]

But first, what exactly is a celebrity? Historian Daniel Boorstin defines a celebrity as a "person well known for their well knownness."[10] This concept of being well known can be translated into celebrity capital defined as the "accumulated media visibility through recurrent media representations."[11] Based on this foundation, celebrities can convert their celebrity capital into economic capital through endorsements.[12] Cultural anthropologist Grant McCracken defined celebrity endorsers as "any individual who enjoys public recognition and who uses this recognition on behalf of a consumer good by appearing with it in an advertisement."[13] But this definition is somewhat dated given that (1) the variety of marketing communication tactics has increased in the past 30 years and (2) the idea of public recognition has changed with the rise of social media, and relatedly, people who are influencers on social media. To take into consideration these changes, a new definition emerged. A celebrity endorsement is "an agreement between an individual who enjoys public recognition (a celebrity) and an entity (e.g., a brand) to use the celebrity for the purpose of promoting the entity."[14]

Given this new conceptualization, the concept of a celebrity and who qualifies as a celebrity is much broader. Both traditional celebrities acting as endorsers and SMIs who are endorsing products hold symbolic capital primarily due to their number of followers and other cues. A key difference is how each gain celebrity capital. Traditional celebrity status is attained outside of endorsements (e.g., independently through prior achievements in a given domain like sports, music, or acting), whereas SMIs center on the Internet and social media by using it to boost their profile.[15] In many cases, SMIs are known for a specific area (e.g., beauty and gaming), and their "knowness" was built online by developing content and a persona on social media platforms such as You Tube, Instagram, and TikTok. Given the ubiquity of social media, marketers need to better understand the differences between celebrity endorsers and SMIs and how best to capitalize on their effectiveness. Researchers have just started to develop a deeper understanding of theories and models from celebrity endorsers that can also shed insight into the effectiveness of SMIs. As such, this attention has led to the explosion of influencer marketing.

Influencer Marketing

While celebrity endorsement has a long and rich research history, influencer marketing—specifically within social media contexts—is much newer. So far, influencer marketing has been under researched,[16] and since influencer marketing is relatively new (at least in the form that it's currently being used), there are several definitions of influencer marketing, from both academic researchers and marketing practitioners. Table 3.1 highlights several definitions of influencer marketing.

When taking all definitions of influencer marketing into consideration, there are several key concepts to consider. First, the concept of influence (e.g., the power to produce an effect without force or command) is central. This influence is often in the form of friendly recommendations through engaging content as opposed to a direct sales pitch. Second, the influencer's existing community of followers is an important target audience for the brand.[17] While follower size (called ties) is important, it is not the only issue to consider. Trust is a key component of the relationship between the influencer and his or her community. Third, since influencers create and share branded content, influencer marketing describes content that exists on social media platforms in a seamless way and is related to branded content and native advertising.[18] Fourth, influencer marketing takes advantage of the fact that influencers typically

Table 3.1 Influencer marketing definitions

Organization	Definition
Hubspot	Influencer marketing is designed to tap into an existing community of engaged followers on social media. Influencers are specialists in their niches. These individuals have influence over an audience you might be trying to reach and can be helpful marketing to those buyers (IZEA The Ultimate Guide to Influencer Marketing)
Buffer	Influencers act as a mutual friend connecting your brand with your target consumers. Moreover, an endorsement from an influencer has the power to drive traffic to your site, amplify your message across social media platforms, and even directly sell your product through their recommendation (IZEA The Ultimate Guide to Influencer Marketing)
Forbes	Influencer marketing should be honest and authentic. An influencer speaks about your product not because they are paid to do so, but because they want to. Ideally, you want an influencer to endorse you because they find your company interesting (IZEA The Ultimate Guide to Influencer Marketing)
Moz	Influencer marketing is the name we give to the process of developing relationships with influential people. Such process can lead to their assisting you in creating visibility for your product or service. This type of marketing depends on your having something great to offer your potential customers and the audience of the influencer, and it also depends on your building a great relationship with the influencer as well (IZEA The Ultimate Guide to Influencer Marketing)
Influencer Marketing Hub	At is most basic, influencer marketing is like a hybrid of old and new marketing tools, taking the idea of the celebrity endorsement and placing it in a modern day, content-driven marketing campaign. Moreover, the main difference is that the results of the campaign are usually collaborations between brands and influencers (IZEA The Ultimate Guide to Influencer Marketing)
IZEA	The process of promoting, selling, or distributing a product or service using indirect or intangible means, or without direct exercise of command (IZEA The Ultimate Guide to Influencer Marketing)
Campbell & Farrell 2020	At its most basic level, influencer marketing is the practice of compensating individuals for posting about a product or service on social media
Yodel 2017	Influencer marketing is a form of marketing where brands invest in selected influencers to create and/or promote their branded content to both the influencer's own followers and the brand's target audiences

have a specific niche(s) that they are known for. This helps them position their content as credible and helps brands identify potential SMIs. Fifth, there are several marketing goals that can be attained using influencer marketing, not only sales. Last, influencer marketing is a form of paid media (as opposed to owned or earned) since influencers are compensated for their content creation and posting on social media. Compensation can be in several forms: money, in kind, or free products, trips, or services.[19] Given this foundation,

> *influencer marketing is the strategy of compensating people who are influential in specific areas to create and promote content on social media on behalf of an organization or brand with content that captures the attention and trust of the influencer's community, thus opening new opportunities for the organization or brand.*

For brands, there are several benefits to adding influencer marketing to the overall marketing strategy. First, influencer marketing content is more organic and authentic than brand-sponsored content. In fact, traditional advertising (print, television) as well as digital advertising (banner ads) has proven to be less effective than in the past and is particularly ineffective with younger audiences. Having influencers generate and distribute content is also an incredibly effective way to design messages that resonate (and provides the brand with quality and trustworthy content that can be repurposed for other needs). Given influencer marketing allows brands to reach a specific, targeted audience—the elusive Generation Z—and allows brand to reach niche audiences that would be difficult to enter without the help of influencers. Second, influencer marketing provides long-term and short-term value. Overall influencer content generates eight times more engagement on social media than brand content. But it depends on the influencer's audience size. Research shows that in many cases as an SMI gains followers they tend to also have lower levels of engagement with them meaning that micro- and nano-influencers who have smaller, more specific audiences may be more beneficial for a brand to reach. Influencer marketing has a high return on investment. A *Tap Influence* Study found that influencer marketing has a return on investment (ROI) that's 11 times greater than other forms of digital marketing and as such, 9 of 10 marketers believe that ROI achieved from influencer marketing is superior to other marketing channels. Third, younger audiences trust and follow advice from SMIs and relate to them more than they relate to traditional celebrities. Last, audiences use SMIs to discover brands which ultimately end up in a purchase.[20]

Social Media Influencers

Social media influencers (SMIs) are also defined in several ways, and despite the recent attention, there is still no standard definition. However, there are several common themes. First, SMIs are a *new type of celebrity endorser* that is different from traditional celebrity endorsers. Sometimes called "micro-celebrities" with large followings on social media platforms,[21] the difference is that *SMIs are seen as regular people* but are also different from the average social media user.[22] This makes SMIs both influential to many, but still seen as "real." Second, SMIs also *command varying audience sizes on social media* platforms such as YouTube, Instagram, Snapchat, TikTok, and blogs but that is extent of their influence sphere for all but the top SMIs. In other words, they built their brand online. Third, SMIs *possess some element of influence and/or opinion leadership capabilities.* Researchers described them as a "new type of third-party endorser who shapes attitudes through … the use of social media to gain earned social capital."[23] SMIs have cultural sway based on their use of their self-branding practices to build this influence.[24] Relatedly, most have *built their reputation and expertise in a few niche areas* and possess specialized knowledge and expertise. Fourth, SMIs *create and disseminate content* and as a result have created a platform where brands can engage with the audience via that SMI. First and foremost, content generators have a status or expertise in a specific area, have cultivated a sizable audience, and have marketing value to brands by regularly producing and disseminating content via social media.[25] Given these themes, SMIs can be defined as "a new type of endorser who creates and disseminates category specific content that is valuable and trusted by his/her community of followers on one more social media platforms and who has the ability to influence that community to act."

As mentioned, SMIs differ from traditional celebrity endorsers. Traditional celebrities have gained their fame through external pursuits such as sports, music, acting, and politics and gain a following through their work, traditional media, and interviews.[26] Not all traditional celebrities (even those who endorse products) have strong social media followings. And reality stars are a particularly interesting case since their fame comes simply through reality television, but most of them maintain a strong social media presence, and as such, they become an SMI in many instances. But typical SMIs are everyday people who develop their personal brand through content creation and engagement with followers that have helped them to become the new brand endorsers based on their perceived credibility, authenticity, and relatability.[27] SMIs tend to have loyal audiences that they earned by carefully cultivating and creating valuable content that inspires, entertains, informs, and connects with their community of followers. They can ultimately drive conversations and engagement and set trends. SMIs have difference audience sizes and reach, rely on a variety of social media channels (although few command equal power on each platform), and work in a variety of categories.[28] SMIs can be known as (1) Instagrammers, (2) YouTubers, (3) Bloggers, (4) TikTokers, (5) Twitch Influencers, and (6) Snapchat influencers. While traditional celebrities can be influencers on social media (and indeed those with the largest followers are in fact traditional celebrities), the focus on most of newer research is gaining a better understand how "regular" people can become effective endorsers online.

Celebrities versus Social Media Influencers versus Brand Ambassadors

Celebrity endorsers, SMIs, and brand ambassadors can all play pivotal roles in marketing strategies. But what is the difference and how can they work? According to a report by Mediakix, brand ambassadors are social media users (can be SMI) who are hired to work collaboratively with companies to promote the brand, introduce new products, and share important information and events. But brand ambassadors are in it for the longer haul—typically working over a larger time span and as such create a deeper relationship with the brand. Brand ambassadors tend to be true advocates of the brand and as such sometimes receive other types of compensation (special event invitations, new products, other opportunities).

(Continued)

In comparison, SMIs typically have a larger reach and have earned the trust of those followers by providing valuable content and interaction with them. Celebrities are known for their work outside of social media and at times lack expertise and genuine connection with their audiences. As a result, marketers have started to move away from celebrity endorsers to designing campaigns with brand ambassadors and/or SMIs.[29] We will explore the use of brand ambassadors in designing a campaign in more depth in Chapter 5.

Influencer Typology

Influencers are generally categorized into two primary tiers—the micro-influencers and macro-influencers.[30] The categories are based on two main issues. First, the number of followers is one way to categorize the influencer types. Second, whether the influencer has influence outside of social media is also an important indicator as to where he or she would land in the influencer category. As the industry has grown in the past few years, it became apparent that there needed to be more structure. The Standard Terminology in Influencer Marketing (STIM) defines tiers of influencers primarily based on their ties with followers (Figure 3.1).

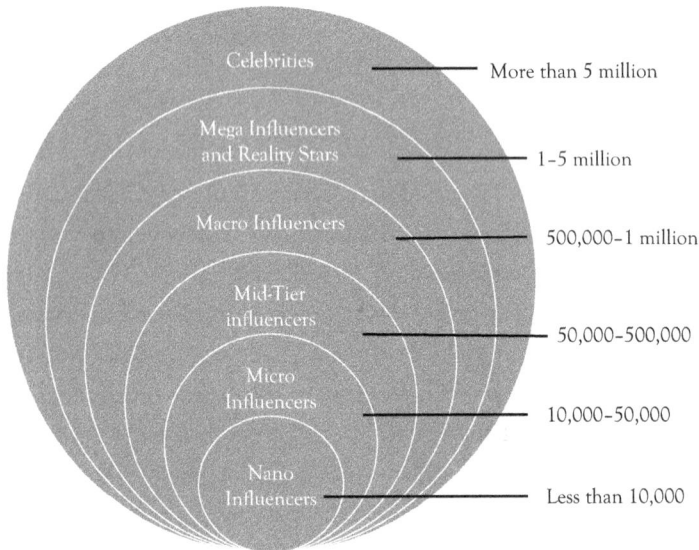

Figure 3.1 Standard terminology in influencer marketing

The top of the influencer pyramid includes celebrities who are well known as athletes, musicians, actors, artists, and other areas. These are typically people with more than five million followers on social media platforms, namely Instagram, TikTok, YouTube, and Twitter. These include top Instagram influencers such as Dwayne "The Rock" Johnson, Kylie Jenner, and Christian Ronaldo. For influencer marketing purposes, someone in the celebrity category should be known for something outside of social media *and* have a large social media following. The celebrity influencer is a natural extension of celebrity endorsers.

Mega Influencers

Mega influencers are those people who are not necessarily known for something outside of social media (but they may be, and as such could be considered minor celebrities). Mega influencers are typically experts in a niche area (e.g., fitness, cooking, and beauty), and social media helped them to become minor celebrities in these areas. Mega influencers are people with between one and five million followers on social media platforms (typically focused on one or two platforms). Examples include many well-known influencers such as Lele Pons for lifestyle, Sommer Ray for fitness, and James Charles for beauty. Mega influencers can also include influencers who are not necessarily tied to an industry niche. These include David Dobrik on YouTube and Charli D'Amelio on TikTok. Others have created channels on YouTube that have large audiences such as Swedish YouTuber PewDiePie who is known for meme reviews and has 102 million subscribers or Ryan's World known for toy reviews with 22.4 million subscribers.

Reality stars are sometimes a special case of mega influencers. Reality stars are like celebrities in that they are famous for something outside of social media. But that is typically for being an "actor" on a reality television or digital show. As part of reality shows, participants also use social media as well, especially as their popularity increases. Many of made the transition from reality star to influencer (e.g., Kim Kardashian and Rachel Lindsay from The Bachelor). For example, Amanda Stanton from the Bachelor franchise has worked with brands like ThredUp, Sperry, Herbal Essence, and Rockbox. Others have used the fame to launch lines and businesses (e.g., Bobby Flay and Teresa Guidice). The primary example is probably the Kardashian/Jenner clan.

Macro-Influencers

Macro-influencers are people with between 500,000 and 1 million followers on social media platforms in a specific niche area. Macro-influencers are used for their large, broad, and diverse audience. Typically, these influencers work across several areas (as opposed to a single niche) and as such can partner with more brands. They are typically part of a larger advertising and branding effort and show higher brand lift and chosen for their visibility. Examples include Whitney Simmons, a top Instagram fitness influencers, and Rachel Levin (RCLBeauty) who shares beauty tips on YouTube.

Mid-Tier Influencers

Mid-tier influencers are typically those with between 50,000 and 500,000 followers who typically have a relatively small niche. These are influencers who fit in between—they don't have as large of an audience as macro-influencers but have larger audiences than micro-influencers. They tend to drive high levels of engagement and are still known for niches. They are in a transition phase—between macro and micro, but given their moderate prices tend to generate positive ROI. Examples include the Old Navy holiday gift giving campaign which partnered with photographer and mid-tier influencer Matt Crump who is known for the #candyminimal movement.

Micro-Influencers

Micro-influencers typically have between 10,000 and 50,000 followers and are local and diverse in their niche areas. They focus on areas such as beauty, travel, and photography and are often found on Instagram. They post consistently and typically create high-quality content. The use of micro-influencers has been popular since they are able to reach small, targeted, and active audiences and tend to be more relatable. However, they do have less reach and lower levels of brand lift. Examples include Florida fashion blogger Chelsea Owen and the Kentucky Gent Josh Johnson who is a lifestyle influencer.

Nano-Influencers

Nano-influencers engage a small audience and typically have been 1,000 and 10,000 followers. Recently, nano-influencers are the sweet spot for brands. These are local and great for small campaigns and local businesses. Typically, nano-influencers personally know almost all their followers and as such have a high level of engagement and authenticity. Additionally, they are inexpensive—in fact, monetary compensation is not as important to them. Consider them like popular friends. They also tend to be easy to recruit and work with. For larger campaigns, brands may be able to deploy hundreds of nano-influencers and be incredibility effective.[31]

Nano-Influencers Make Major Impact

Influencer marketing has typically been associated with people with thousands or several hundreds of thousands of followers on social media. These mega, macro-, and mid-tier influencers also come with a price. Some brands are opting out. Johnson & Johnson is placing bets on smaller influencers—nano-influencers. Clean & Clear enlisted a handful of teens with fewer than 1,000 followers. Simon Geraghty, U.S. acne portfolio lead for Johnson & Johnson, told AdAge the "brand is placing its bets on influencers who aren't famous per se but are doing things that other kids respond to authentically, letting them tell their story and building the products and brands from there." One such influencer was Dillon Eisman, 18, who runs a nonprofit in California that restores damaged apparel for homeless teens who had fewer than 1,000 followers. Brands are betting that these teens will resonate when social media has a ton of fake followers, and many are questioning how real they even are. It worked! Clean & Clear's sales jumped 19 percent since its launch.[32]

Employees

One special type of employees that don't specifically fall into traditional categories include a company's employees and leadership. Some companies are beginning to create and leverage employees in so-called employee advocate programs. However, this is still in its infancy. There could be some legal issues involved for some brands. But for those companies who can, tapping employees can be an amazing way to expand the brand's community. Think about it—employees already have brand affinity and can speak with authority in an authentic way. And each has a social media following of various sizes and engagement. But more importantly, employees hold a unique position since brand impressions are largely the result of interactions with people.

Using employees as influencers can provide a few ways to try things and experiment, especially for smaller, local brands who are in service business.[33] One such example is West Gissinger in Dallas, Texas (@westgissinger on Instagram). She has 5,292 followers and is a Pilates instructor at Session Pilates. She posts about Sessions and her ab attack routine and works with a few other fitness brands. "Part of being a successful fitness professional is being active on social media. It comes with the territory. In boutique fitness, once you have earned your class spots you have gained a platform and it is up to each fitness professional to use it how they want to his or her advantage," said West Gissinger. "Social media is one of the easiest and most direct ways to create excitement around the classes I teach as well as the other events at the studio. I use my social media to communicate my weekly class schedule, educate people on proper form, show what reformer Pilates is all about, ask for feedback or movement requests, and pull back the curtain on who I am beyond being on the microphone." She also added that social media training is part of the instructor training and Sessions expect its instructors to post across social media. Sessions give employees a lot of creative freedom to do that. "Your instructors are our biggest brand ambassadors," said Gissinger. "They are walking, talking, living, breathing embodiment of the brand."[34]

For business-to-consumer sectors, a great example is the Peloton instructors discussed in the following box. In fact, for many people, the instructors are Peloton. In this case, the Peloton instructors have amassed thousands of followers on Instagram with high engagement levels which contributes to the overall vibrancy of the community. Additionally, Peloton has spawned people who create audiences based on love for Peloton. The Pelobuddy on Instagram is a good example. The Pelobuddy set up the account to follow and post news about Peloton like new instructors, new features, and reposts from One Peloton, the official Instagram account as well as from instructor account.

Peloton: How a Company Was Built by Leveraging Its Own Influencers

One of the fitness industry's biggest names is Peloton, a company who knows the power of influencers and also how to create them. Since launching in 2012 (via a Kickstarter campaign—so social media is in the DNA), the home fitness company that produces the Peloton indoor cycle and Peloton Tread has rocketed to pop culture status (and financial stardom). Which is interesting given the premise of the company. Instead of going to a local gym to take boutique fitness classes, consumers purchase a bike for $2,200 or treadmill for $4,000 and pay a monthly subscription fee. But the real recipe to success is the community of instructors (who have become major influencers on social media in their own right) as well as the millions of Peloton enthusiasts (who have also transferred some of their love for Peloton into influencer success). Some of the Peloton fitness instructors are truly members of the creator economy (e.g., Alex Toussiant, one of the most popular cycle instructors launched his own clothing brand) and provide excellent examples of a brand using their own employees as influencers and advocates. Instructors have amassed a huge following based on the authentic connections they start in class (whether in person, live, or on demand) and finish on Instagram. Top instructor SMIs include Robin Arzon, Kristin McGee, Chase Tucker, Denis Morton, Alex Toussaint, and Ally Love, but most instructors saw massive increases in the number of followers during the global pandemic since people could not go to gyms. Peloton saw its sales soar. Peloton's 2020 revenue was $1.8 billion.

In particular, Peloton uses branded apparel and encourages instructors to connect with followers online in order to share stories that they can't always explore during class. This maximizes the idea of a "real-life" relationship between customers and instructors—much like it would be in person. The strategy builds a strong community while also amplifying the brand.[37]

For business-to-business (B2B) sectors, influencers can be clients, employees, or CEOs. Companies such as Prudential Financial and Cisco have leveraged employee advocacy programs.[35] Salesforce is a great example of a B2B who maximizes the influence of CEO Marc Benioff who is very active on Twitter. In 2015, IBM created an influencer program that allowed employees to share content on their social media platforms.[36] Regardless, though, the content must be more authentic and less promotional that with traditional influencers.

Everyday Fans

Many brands are realizing the value of their customers as influencers. For some brands, they are downright fans! Brian Salzman, the founder and CEO of relationship marketing agency RQ, said "the fan is the ultimate influencer, and leveraging their power is the best influencer marketing tactic around."[38] Emily Weiss of Glossier (see Chapter 2 for her story) knows the value of using their own customers as influencers. In addition to using traditional influencers (e.g., Beyonce), Glossier also created an engaged community of fans who are now formal representatives (e.g., brand ambassadors) who endorse the brand on social media and IRL (in real life). Glossier's only requirement is that they share values and produce content that the brand likes and who have something interesting to say about the products. They also want people from diverse backgrounds and locations. Their program has grown from 11 girls to more than 500. Other brands such as Peloton, Kylie Cosmetics, and the Ordinary are others who have tapped the power of community as influencers.[39]

Influencer Selection

So, how does a marketing manager select the best option? Each influencer tier has advantages and disadvantages depending on the brand and goals for the campaign. If a brand is trying to reach a mass audience, it makes sense to use mega or macro-influencers (provided there is enough budget). Micro- and nano-influencers tend to have high levels of engagement with audiences and as such tend to have a lot of loyalty. Some brands use a mix of several influencer types based on campaign goals. As stated earlier, more and more brands are looking to micro- and nano-influencers given engagement rates and costs.

But is this system even the best way to categorize influencers? Doubtful. There is a lack of consensus on how many tiers there should be and how they are defined. It is also important to understand that simple quantitative measures like number of followers (or ties representing degree or centrality) or the ratio of vanity metrics such as likes, shares, comments to the total base (frequently used to measure engagement) cannot be the only consideration when selecting an influencer or evaluating a campaign.[40] Neal Shaffer argues that brand affinity is another way to differentiate influencers. The first level of brand affinity is employees. Customers and fans are the second level and last, and influencers are the last tier of brand affinity.[41] He argues that in some cases, the first level of brand affinity is the most effective and then goes down from there. Some research examines influence in a more macro-way referring to "perceived opinion leadership," leaving even more confusion on how to measure influencers. Research shows that influencers who follow fewer people convey a greater sense of autonomy which is seen as a positive signal of influence.[42] Findings vary from a clear connection of followers and opinion leadership[43] to the number of followers simply being a proxy for popularity rather than influence.[44] So, this issue is still open for debate.

Platforms and Industry Categories

There are hundreds of social media platforms (and more being created regularly). Some come and go (remember Vine?). Some platforms are better for influencers (e.g., Instagram) than others (e.g., Snapchat). As platforms rise and fall, from a marketing perspective, the most important thing is to understand how people use social media platforms, what they do on them, and what content is best suited for platforms. Currently, people use social media platforms to (1) communicate and socialize with family and friends, (2) communicate and socialize with people unknown people but with whom there is a shared or comment interest, and (3) access and contribute to news and opinions (through user-generated content). Each of these cases represents a form of WOM marketing.[45]

Currently, the top social media platforms for influencer marketing are Instagram, YouTube, and TikTok. All three of these platforms share traits in common—all visually based (photos or videos), all are open where it is easy to find influencers and follow, and the content remains on the site. Contrast that with Snapchat where the communication is more intimate between friends and is not automatically archived on the site. Facebook, while it is still the largest platform (and maybe because of it), does find itself in the same influencer category. On Facebook, content can take on several forms. LinkedIn is an interesting case as well. While it may not have the pop culture attention, people in business use it to create and disseminate "thought leadership" which can be considered a specific type of influence.

Most influencers—especially nano- and micro-influencers—have a primary social media platform. Currently, YouTube, Instagram, TikTok, and Twitch dominate the landscape. Some influencers do distribute their content across multiple platforms, but typically their influence is not equal across all of them. This is primarily due to the nature of the platforms, and how each matches influencer content. Instagram has highly visual, curated content with some video through Instagram Stories and IGTV. Influencers on Instagram are primarily lifestyle, fitness, beauty, and travel. YouTube and YouTube creators focus on longer form video, which is best for comedy, beauty (especially "how to" videos), automotive, technology, and lifestyle. Bloggers create long-form written and visual content, and platforms like Medium and SubStack are growing. Twitch is primarily livestreamed gaming and TikTok is short-form video.

There are several product and brand categories that use influencer marketing. And more types of brands are getting in. Some of these categories make a lot of sense. For example, beauty and fashion brands have used celebrities and models for years, so the addition of SMIs is a natural extension. The top niches for influencers include beauty, fashion, travel, luxury, lifestyle, parenting, health and fitness, and pets and animals. Brands can then connect with influencers in these categories that make the most sense for their goals. Table 3.2 outlines several of the categories where brands connect with influencers.

Nonprofit organizations are also able to use influencer marketing effectively. There are several examples of celebrities using their platforms for good. Emma Watson is a UN Women Goodwill Ambassador and Orlando Bloom is a UNICEF Goodwill Ambassador. But other nonprofits have tapped noncelebrities too. WWF partnered with travel photographers for their campaign #Toolatergram where the photographers posted photos of natural beauty spots that have already been affected by climate change. During the pandemic, influencers were also able to provide support for parents facing similar challenges. This was in collaboration with

Table 3.2 Key categories for influencer marketing

Category	
Gaming	Video game livestreams, E-sports, player tips, unboxing consoles, gaming product reviews
Family	Parents and family, relationship advice
Health and fitness	Fitness, yoga/meditation, health, wellness
Fashion and beauty	Luxury, clothing, styling, makeup tutorials, makeovers
Home	Luxury, styling, makeovers
Technology	Technology reviews; how to guide
Travel	Travel, backpackers, adventurers, photographers
Automotive	Car enthusiasts, auto repair guides
Music and entertainment	Singer, songwriter, musician, bands, videos, reviews of movies, shows, music
Finance and insurance	Banking and personal finance advice, investing advice, insurance advice
Pharmaceuticals and other regulated industries	Medical information about drugs and recently vaccines

UNICEF and WHO.[46] The process for influencer marketing with non-profits is essentially the same. However, the compensation issues may be different. According to Addi McCauley of IZEA, "when nonprofits are working with influencers a lot of times they are not necessarily paying influencers like brands have to. Essentially the influencer is saying 'I care about the cause and I want to partner with you because I have a platform to help spread your message.'" The challenge for nonprofits is that many times they want to equate influencer marketing with donations and that does not always happen. "Influencer marketing is not at its core a direct response marketing tactic, so I think a lot of it is more about the storytelling. It works better when the influencer brings it to their network versus the other way around," McCauley added.[47]

As more brands capitalize on influencer marketing strategies, brand managers need to know more about how to design effective campaigns and how about they work. While is important to understand the "what" behind influencer marketing campaigns, academic research attempts to examine the deeper questions of "why" and "how" influencer marketing works. The next chapter examines this research so that marketers can get a solid foundation for their strategic decisions.

Fake or Real? Artificial Intelligence and Social Media Endorsers

Just when you thought you had heard it all, along comes artificial intelligence (AI) influencers. AI influencers are defined as a "digitally created artificial human who is associated with Internet fame and uses software and algorithms to perform tasks like humans."[48] Examples include Lil Miquela, Bermuda, and Blawko which are ranked as some of the top virtual influencers on Instagram. They are created to have distinct humanlike visual likeness. In fact, Lil Miquela was named as one of *Time Magazine's* most influential people on the Internet in 2018 (despite that she is not human). At the time, she promoted luxury brands such as Prada and Balenciago.[49] At first glance, these AI endorsers seem attractive to marketers, not the least of which is because they are unlikely to be involved in a scandal. AI influencers are evaluated and benefit a brand in a similar way to celebrity endorsers. And they commit transgressions just like human SMIs. Research shows that regardless of whether an endorser is an AI influencer or celebrity, when the endorser commits a transgression has a negative effect on the brand. Additionally, virtual SMIs can have unintended consequences. AI influencers can become attuned to followers' personalities and then use this information to better inform ways to interact—this potentially using data for questionable purposes.

CHAPTER 4

Celebrity Endorsers and Social Media Influencers

How It Works

Using Influencers to Destigmatize Mental Health

The app Headspace has a mission to "improve the health and happiness of the world." Headspace is there to guide and partner with people on their mental health journey and tries to destigmatize mental health issues while also providing the benefits of things like meditation. This became increasingly important as the pandemic hit in 2020, and anxiety levels hit all-time high for many people. And while the destigmatization was happening before Covid, it was accelerated. Additionally, people got much more comfortable with digital products in the health space. Now people are returning to normal, albeit a new normal, by establishing new routines and new habits.

Headspace worked with influencer marketing agency Collectively to design a content creator strategy. The campaign focused on Headspace's sleep products, where the goal was to increase consideration of the app. During the pandemic, mental health became an interesting issue as some celebrities did not show much empathy and connection with everyday people. But some influencers did understand it and had authentic ways to bring empathy into content. One influencer was Chrissy Rutherford, who is a fashion and social media expert. She said that she has been a huge fan and user of Headspace for years, so when she partnered with them, her audience felt a seamless connection. "Headspace gave me the freedom to tell my story and how it resonates with me," she said. She developed authentic content around it and experimented with new formats like Instagram's Reels and also used Stories. It was important for the brand to loosen control on the content for this campaign, which Headspace easily did. Influencers were chosen based on how they were able to discuss the topic in an honest and vulnerable way. Collectively did a lot of research to identify the best options and also created a double opt in so that influencers were verified users of Headspace.

Success was measured in a variety of ways. Of course, the numbers play an important role, but Headspace also examined the online conversations in more depth and looked at whether the audiences were getting into the topic. This campaign showed that brands are welcoming authentic, relatable, and human dialogue to stand out.[1]

How Influencer Marketing Works

While the research on influencer marketing and SMIs is in its infancy, the research on celebrity endorsers—and indeed, endorsement in general—has a long history. Several key theories from that research foundation may be used to explain "how" influencer marketing may work. This insight helps marketing managers to understand the underlying mechanisms which inform their decisions about campaign goals and objectives, influencer selection, campaign structure, and performance measurement. This insight also assists researchers to identify the major gaps in the literature as well as differences in traditional celebrities and SMIs as to how they affect consumer behavior. This chapter includes an overview of the major theories and what was learned within a celebrity endorsement context, what has been learned in an SMI context, and what gaps still exist when attempting to understand influencer marketing. Key theories include source credibility and source effects (including source attractiveness), matchup hypothesis/congruence, and the meaning transfer model.

Source Credibility and Source Effects

One of the most important questions to ask is how an endorser persuades someone to act. In other words, why that endorser? What makes he or she special? Source credibility (and relatedly source effects) is probably one of the most researched theories to explain how endorsers work.[2] Source credibility is commonly used to understand how a communicator's positive characteristics affects the receiver's acceptance of that message.[3]

While there are various contexts where source credibility is important as well as several ways to measure it, the most relevant definition relates to endorsers. Two conceptual models form that foundation: the source-credibility model,[4] which highlights the importance of expertise and trustworthiness, and the source-attractiveness model[5] which adds attractiveness, which depends on the source's familiarity, similarity, likability, and attractiveness to the respondent. Early research[6] defined source credibility as primarily a function of expertise, trustworthiness, and attractiveness. This model tends to be the most popular conceptualization of source credibility in the celebrity endorser literature. Specifically, source credibility is defined as follows:

- Expertise, which is based on the degree to which the consumer sees the endorser as experienced, knowledgeable, qualified, or skilled in a specific area.
- Trust, which is based on how well the consumer has confidence in and acceptance of the messages from the endorser.
- Attractiveness, which is based on the consumer perceptions of beauty, elegance, sexiness, and physical attractiveness of the endorser.

Figure 4.1 highlights the components of source credibility.

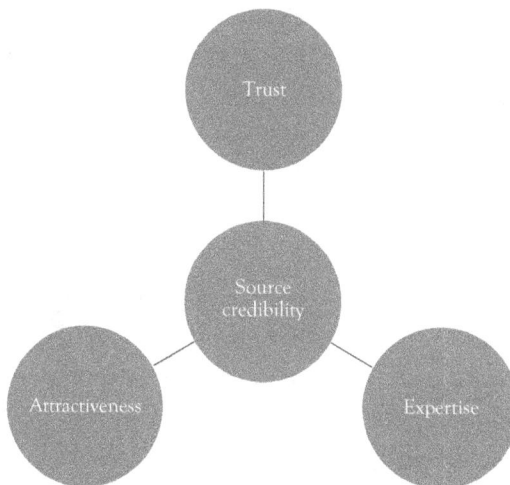

Figure 4.1 Source credibility

Generally, it is assumed that celebrities who are attractive, credible, and trustworthy should yield positive consumer evaluations of the brand. However, it is rarely that simple. The research on the effect of celebrity endorsements on brand evaluations *generally* finds that persuasion is higher when expertise and attractiveness is high. Interestingly, trustworthiness has mixed effects on brand evaluations with some showing little to no effect,[7] whereas some research has shown a positive effect of trustworthiness[8] especially for low involvement consumers.[9] It has been argued that the low trust could be a result of consumers knowing that celebrities are paid. The role of expertise is also mixed; some show the positive impact of expertise,[10] whereas other research found a delayed, but not direct impact of expertise.[11] The impact of expertise depends on the product type[12] and on consumer type.[13]

There is a long history of research of marketing, beauty and attractiveness.[14] Much the relevant work regarding attractiveness occurred between the mid-1970s and mid-1990s that acknowledged the power of attractiveness.[15] But, physical attractiveness can also include other attributions such as likeability, familiarity, and liking.[16] In many cases, recognition and celebrity status mattered more than physical attractiveness.[17] Results are mixed when examining levels of celebrity liking (there have been few studies examining this specifically) and role of celebrity-brand fit.[18] All said, there has been important research to show the power of source credibility and celebrity endorsers.

What about SMIs? The research on the effects of source credibility and source effects for SMI persuasion is relatively new. But researchers have started to shed light on how source credibility theories can be applied to SMIs and their effects on brand evaluations. Here is what we know.

Trust

Given that SMIs have a strong relationship with their followers, trust should play an important role in persuasion, especially those who are SMIs rather than celebrities.[19] In fact, some research shows that trust was more important for SMIs than for celebrities in one of the only studies to directly compare the two endorser types.[20] Trust has a positive effect on brand evaluations,[21] and trust was higher when there was product fit with the influencer.[22] One issue that perhaps is of importance is the relationship between the influencer and followers, as well as who the influencer follows back. Research has examined the potential effects of trust and credibility by looking at the ratio of followers versus people the influencer follows in the assessment of an SMI. They found that this ratio matters and called for more investigation into whether a high number of followers (and a low number of accounts the SMI follows) could cause consumers to question whether the SMI is fact "real" and not a fake account.[23] Obviously, this has the potential to degrade trust. Other research found no relationship of trustworthiness on product interest.[24] There is some speculation that followers may be skeptical of the motives of even a trustworthy SMI.

All of that said, influencer marketing can be used to encourage trust. Trust can be a result of similarity (she or she is like me) or aspirational (I want to be like that person). Influencer marketing agency IZEA created a campaign with the Commonwealth of Kentucky called the "Mask Up KY Initiative." The campaign used native Kentuckians at various influencer levels (nano-influencers to macro-influencers) across all social media platforms. The goal was to create content that spurred positive conversations about mask wearing during the pandemic (before the vaccine). The campaign also demonstrated how neighbors can stick together toward a common goal. This highlighted the impact of trust and influencers. The campaign results were 216 pieces of created content, 15 million people reached, and 38 million impressions at a cost of 83 cents per engagement.[25]

Expertise

Expertise is an important criterion since most SMIs fit into a specialized genre or category based on their interests.[26] Perceptions of expertise was higher when there was product fit between the brand and the influencer.[27] But it was not that simple. Other research found no effect of expertise on brand evaluations, from either SMIs or celebrities[28] or on product interest.[29] Given that SMIs tend to create content in specific categories, more clarity on the role of expertise is warranted especially whether there is a difference based on the type of endorser (e.g., monomorphic vs. polymorphic).

Practically, however, expertise is important for some product categories. Cetaphil is a popular mass skincare brand. Research conducted by the brand found that 70 percent of Americans self-diagnose sensitive skin issues like dryness, irritation, and roughness. As such, Cetaphil launched a week-long campaign "Sensitive Skin Awareness Week in March 2021" and capitalized on DermTok,[30] a growing trend where dermatologists post videos to educate millions of people about skincare issues and try to debunk misguided ideas about skincare. Called skinfluencers, they have made a huge impact in the skincare space on social media. One top skinfluencer is skincare by Hyram, who has created videos on YouTube.

"Skinfluencers have really shifted the way that the skincare market and brands work with influencers. They used to have celebrities—like Jennifer Aniston—but now brands are shifting and saying that celebrities are not driving brand consideration and that influencers and dermatologists on social media that back our products are driving the market," said Andrea Arias, associate brand manager for Cetaphil. Cetaphil aligned with a few of these dermatologists—Edward Zo and Melissa Alatorre—who are popular on TikTok and Instagram. "We saw a shift in the way that consumers are purchasing products and the way that we as brands think about brand consideration, so we did the first TikTok campaign to test and learn," said Arias. "We split the campaign into two using skinfluencers and lifestyle influencers that were in the beauty category and who had some original content around it and ran the campaign October and November 2020." This partnership with expert influencers has helped Cetaphil rise in popularity from number four to number three, primarily due to the interest of Generation Z and skincare. "Generation Z are very much skintellectuals and this has been reflected in the slowing of cosmetic sales and the increase of skin care," said Claire Varge, head of beauty at WGSN. Cetaphil launched its first TikTok influencer campaign tapping 23 people to spotlight its cleaners. They also boosted the content. The fact that many of these influencers are experts emphasizes that the idea of expertise crucial criteria for some brands and campaigns.[31] Arias added that "the campaign drove brand consideration of cleaners and we saw a spike in sales, and we saw positive metrics on our website. So, it was a good indicator that being in new platforms like TikTok is valuable."[32]

Influencer Marketing During the Covid-19 Pandemic

The pandemic affected everything. And we saw two main issues. First, influencers played a major role in disseminating health information during the pandemic and continues to play a role in encouraging vaccinations. Recent initiatives showed the intersection of public health and influencer marketing. One of the many challenges of the pandemic was to deploy accurate and trusted information to the masses. But people don't trust traditional sources. In fact, one survey showed that only 42 percent trusted government sources about the pandemic. And this was especially true for marginalized communities. Influencers (at all levels) were able to meet this challenge showing the power of trust and expertise. Entities from government and health departments to vaccine manufacturers and pharmacies have partnered with influencers to reach niche audiences. Organizations focused on messaging like the science, safety, and availability of testing and vaccines. Influencers create, share, amplify, and repurpose content regarding health behavior.[33]

Second, we saw that brands can be creative when faced with constraints. The pandemic really put a damper on new brand launches, especially those that require some amount of in person engagement. Riot Games launched its first new game in 10 years called Valorant into a very crowded gaming space. The Riot team had to get major gaming influencers on board, and they were able to have an in person event in January 2020 when it was still called Project A. They were planning to launch in February 2020 with several events and more than 300 of the top gamers in the world. Obviously, that did not happen. Riot Games then moved the whole launch online and learned a few key lessons. First, it was a massive success because they made it really easy for their creators to create content for themselves. Second, they learned that the security risk—of letting a prerelease of a game out to 300 people on their personal computers—was worth it. "We created an ecosystem for creators to keep engaging with our brand," said Ali Miller, global influencer program lead for Riot Games. "Relationships matter."[34]

Attractiveness

It is no secret that many SMIs are attractive. In fact, for many (most), their looks played a direct role in their popularity. Early research examined the role of attractiveness and how it relates to brand evaluations and found that marketing managers should consider attractiveness when selecting SMIs (especially in relationship to the brand/product image). They found that attractiveness influences the perceived fit between the influencer and brand.[35] However, other research found no effect of attractiveness.[36]

This indicates that more examination is needed in exactly what attractiveness is and means for SMIs, especially when there are other factors, such as authenticity at play. For celebrity endorsers, there is more to attractiveness so assuming at least some similarities, and diving deeper into the concept of attractiveness, there are other variables that are important to SMIs.

Liking

One aspect of attractiveness (and perhaps a large factor in the effectiveness of influence) is liking. In other words, is the endorser likable to audiences and potential customers? De Veirman and colleagues examined cues around popularity and opinion leadership. They found that the number of followers that an SMI has does affect consumers' attitudes toward him or her by tapping into the issue of likability.[37] This is primarily explained by perceptions of popularity and in line with previous research, but it remains unclear whether liking translates into real opinion leadership (or influence). More research is needed on the role of liking for SMIs.

Identification and Similarity

Another consideration is the issue of identification or similarity. Seemingly this is one reason that SMIs are popular—that audiences can identify with them and can see themselves with them. Research shows that this does hold true. When examining other issues related to source credibility, consumers identified more with SMIs, felt more similar with them than celebrities, and were more willing to purchase from SMI.[38] But not much research has tackled the issue of identification, so more research is needed on the importance of similarity and identification between the SMI and his or her audience.

Despite that initiatives with SMIs are relatively new, there has been some strong research to examine how effective SMIs can be for brand building. However, there are several important gaps in understanding how SMIs can build brands. The bottom line is that more attention is needed. What do we need to learn? Well, trustworthiness was generally not important when using celebrity endorsers, but it would seem to be important to SMIs since they have closer and more trust-based relationships with their community. Additionally, the role of liking and the role of attractiveness may prove to be different with SMIs compared to celebrity endorsers. Specifically, these two variables could be prove to be more (liking) or less (attractiveness) important for SMIs than celebrity endorsers. One concept that is missing from celebrity endorsements is the role of authenticity. Given the differences between celebrities and SMIs, what (if any) is the role of authenticity for SMIs? This seems to be important for SMIs but is not considered for celebrity endorsers. Last, given why SMIs are chosen, are there other variables to consider? More on that later. But before we do, let's look at a few other theories that are important to celebrity endorsement and could prove useful to influencer marketing. Figure 4.2 highlights the components of source attractiveness.

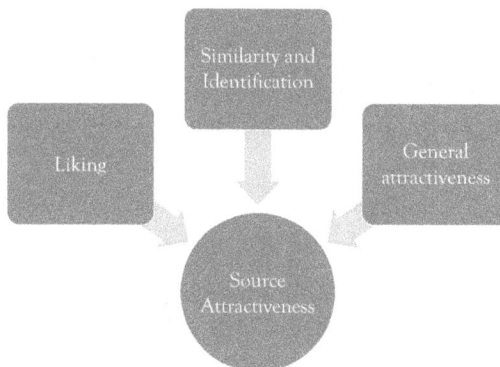

Figure 4.2 Aspects of source attractiveness

Match Up Hypothesis and the Role of Congruence

Early research on the impact of source credibility (trust, expertise, and attractiveness specifically) suggests that any celebrity who fits this description can endorse a product effectively.[39] This has been challenged because it does not explain why some endorsers are more or less effective than others. This led to research on the match up hypothesis, which suggested that an endorser would be most effective if there was "congruence" or "fit" among the endorser, product, and target audience. In other words, there should be a way that they match up to create effective persuasion. The process underlying the matchup hypothesis can be explained with social adaptation theory[40] and schema theory.[41] Both assume that congruence will yield positive effects on brand evaluations. Congruence consists of relevancy, defined as the "degree to which the information held in the celebrity endorser contributes a clear, lucid representation of the communicated theme,"[42] and expectancy, defined as the degree to which stimuli fit some expected pattern or theme. Congruence is dependent on the specific situation—the product and the endorser in each situation. Research has shown that when consumers feel that there is a match between the endorser and the product, it results in more positive brand evaluations.[43] In fact, the issue of congruence can be so important that it has effects on other variables in both direct and indirect ways.[44] Other research took a more holistic view of image and congruence.[45] While the results are mixed, generally higher congruence is more effective than lower congruence.

The matchup hypothesis has been used to examine SMIs. Matchup is important to both the brand and the SMI. The concept of matchup is particularly important for SMIs given they regularly communicate with their followers, establishing relationships and para-social interactions (discussed later in this chapter).[46] Much of the communication between SMI and their followers is not persuasive in nature; so, to maintain trust and authenticity, SMIs need to be careful about who they partner with and what they say in messaging. But what about the relationship with followers? It can also be argued that given the "special characteristics of social media influencers might diminish the importance of the perceived fit" thus developing a halo effect due to the nature of para-social relationships.

Research shows that matchup between the SMI and brand has a positive impact on the image of the SMI and brand evaluations, thus showing that even for the SMI, congruence is important. Researchers argued this is important given that when reaching out to new audiences, some brands choose SMIs that may not be good fits for their brands. They found that congruence is important for perceptions of expertise and trustworthiness for the endorser as well. SMIs need to consider their fit with brands to avoid damaging their relationships with followers. If they do happen to work with a brand that is slightly incongruent, SMIs need to create a personal post to generate para-social interaction.[47]

That said, in a direct comparison between SMIs and celebrities, some researchers have found that contrary to expectations about the role of fit, they did not find any relationship. Fit did not explain the relationship between type of endorser (SMI vs. celebrity) and expertise or trust.[48] Despite the lack of a relationship, they did find that respondents identified with more, felt more liking, and trusted SMIs over than celebrities, showing the potential for SMIs as effective brand endorsers.

Meaning Transfer Model

While the previous theoretical foundation of source credibility and match up hypothesis are important, these do not capture the endorser's broader cultural meaning.[49] In this model, the endorser (in earlier cases, the celebrity) was part of the broader pop culture and brought some of that to the endorser-brand relationship. The aim was to demonstrate the transfer of nonevaluative traits from the celebrity to the brand.[50] Cultural anthropologist Grant McCracken argues celebrities provide meaning through their work and their celebrity status. Audiences respond to the endorser's identity based on both evaluative and nonevaluative traits, which is accumulated over time through their performances. As such, these traits are persuasive because they represent broader meanings.[51] There is not necessarily an explicit relationship between the celebrity meanings and the product since they are created through symbolic cues and advertising. But consumers then recognize the cultural meanings in both the product and the endorser and "transfer meaning" between the two. If this transfer happens, endorser-brand relationships can be really effective. A great example is Nike and Michael Jordan. Michael Jordan is a great basketball player known around the globe. When he began a deep, decades long relationship in the 1980s with shoe brand Nike, who was trying to establish itself in basketball, the relationship not only proved to be amazing from a consumer perspective but was worth millions to Nike's bottom line. Interestingly, despite being one of the most widely cited articles, only a few studies have attempted to test McCracken's meaning transfer model.[52] Newer research has extended the meaning transfer model to the process transfer model, suggesting that the way consumers evaluate an endorser may be more sophisticated given the variety of both celebrities and SMIs that are used.[53] It attempts to supplement existing models to provide a more comprehensive understanding of endorser effects. Other research used meaning transfer to examine the effect of attractiveness and congruence between the SMI and the brand and found positive evaluations of the brand. This research shows that both attractiveness and congruence are important to evaluation effectiveness and shows that this congruence facilitates meaning transfer from the SMI to the brand.[54]

Overall, there are several key theories from celebrity endorsement research that can be explored to shed additional light on how influencer marketing works. That said, given the unique nature of SMIs relative to traditional celebrities—specifically that they build their brand completely online, at least initially—there are several other key theories that need more examination. Additionally, it is important to understand more about the audience. Who are they? What works best with them? Are there differences across gender, ages, other variables? Given that influencer marketing is particularly effective with younger audiences, how should SMIs build their following that maximizes their connections with their followers, specifically with millennials and Generation Z?

Generation Z and SMIs: Understanding Followers and Fans

Influencer marketing has changed how brands promote their products and services, and this new strategy is particularly effective with two audiences—millennials (aged 25–40) and Generation Z (13–24). More than three quarters of both generational cohorts follow influencers on social media and most say that this is the way to learn about new products. A *Morning Consult* Survey shows that both men and women are influenced by SMIs. In terms of topics, men prefer gaming and sports influencers, while women prefer beauty and fashion. They all follow influencers on social media for four primary reasons: inspiration and aspiration; voyeurism; to learn about trends; and they find them interesting and fun. Important traits about influencers include (very important + somewhat important):

- Authenticity 88 percent
- Funny and engaging 88 percent
- Knowledgeable 85 percent
- Intelligent and thoughtful 83 percent
- Interests similar to me 83 percent
- Good taste and trust recommendations 78 percent

Other traits included attractiveness-related traits such as personal and open, beautiful images, and physically attractive. Interestingly, having a large following was least important (29 percent). So, it is easy to see the connections between what is important to this audience and the characteristics of source credibility discussed earlier.

Millennials and Generation Z also act on recommendations from SMIs. This is how 88 percent of them learn about products and 56 percent have made a purchase directly due to an SMI post. They also trust an influencer's recommendations about products. While friends and family are still the most trusted sources to give advice, SMIs are ranked higher in trust than celebrities. Knowledge is also an important characteristic in the effectiveness of SMIs. In terms of social media platforms, YouTube is more popular with men while Instagram reigns supreme with women.

Interestingly, many young Americans want to be influencers! Fifty four percent said they would become an influencer if given the opportunity and 12 percent already consider themselves to be one. Sixty-six percent they would be willing to post sponsored content for money, especially when it comes to travel, events, and memes but primarily if they liked the product. Figure 4.3 illustrates a description of Generation Z.

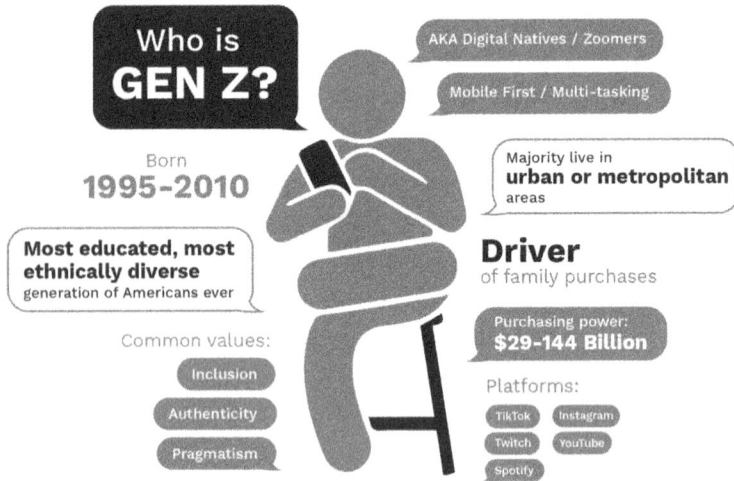

Who is
GEN Z?

AKA Digital Natives / Zoomers

Mobile First / Multi-tasking

Born
1995-2010

Majority live in
urban or metropolitan
areas

**Most educated, most
ethnically diverse**
generation of Americans ever

Driver
of family purchases

Common values:

Inclusion

Authenticity

Pragmatism

Purchasing power:
$29-144 Billion

Platforms:

TikTok   Instagram

Twitch   YouTube

Spotify

Figure 4.3 Generation Z[55]

Given the importance of SMIs to this audience, there has been little attention on the effect of target audience factors on celebrity persuasion and SMI impact. Earlier research on celebrities found no age-related differences in the audience's perceptions of them. However, that research did not consider the new definition of celebrities and the role of social media. This is important given that SMIs are most popular with millennials and Generation Z, who don't seem to differentiate the concept of a "traditional" celebrity from that of SMIs. Research on gender differences with celebrity persuasion has also been mixed and limited. Additionally, no studies really examine cross-cultural differences, or race/ethnicity differences, or whether and how celebrities and SMIs can persuade consumers and where those differences may lie. So, what do we know about how SMIs develop engaging relationships with their followers?

Connecting SMIs and Their Followers

The influencer's relationship with the audience is the most valuable element when brands consider SMI selection. The personal nature of social media enables celebrities and influencers to initiate a quasi, two-way relationship with followers. This is quite different from the top down, one-way communication between celebrities and audience through mass media like television and movies. An important part of social media is that it enables users to interact with SMIs and brands through likes, shares, and comments that seem to create a sense of friendship. While the interaction is far from reciprocal and differs from how people would interact with friends and family, the idea of being closer to SMIs is one major difference in the current ways that endorsement works. And SMIs tend to spend more time cultivating those relationships since their brand is built entirely online. These are called para-social relationships. Para-social relationships[56] have been studied in various contexts (e.g., television hosts, soap opera stars, and movie stars). This is essentially where an audience member (or follower in this case) feels a connection to a media personality (in this case, an SMI). It is an intimate relationship—a socioemotional bond that occurs that is now more easily facilitated due to the nature of social media platforms and the ubiquity of social media usage.[57] Recently, multiple studies have examined the para-social relationships between social media users and SMIs[58] and report strong para-social relationships between audience and their favorite SMIs, especially with higher levels of online social interaction.

Para-social relationships are an important concept when examining the influence of SMIs. Researchers[59] investigated the determinants and role of source credibility in para-social relationships between SMIs and their followers, as well as their followers' interests in the products endorsed by the influencer. Specifically, followers' perceived attractiveness and perceived similarity to the influencer and fairness with how influencers communicated with followers positively affected the strength of these para-social relationships between SMI and followers. It also increases their interest in endorsed products. Interestingly, perceived expertise and trustworthiness did not relate to the strength of para-social relationships. Perhaps, being an expert or being trustworthy did not seem to help cultivate this type of relationship between the SMI and followers. Practically, the effect of para-social relationships can be powerful. Addi McCauley of IZEA has seen campaigns where audiences feel very close to the influencer treating and communicating with them like friends. "Personally, after the birth of my daughter, I follow a postpartum nurse from St. Louis. She constantly posts about mom tips and mom hacks and is constantly posting where people have direct messaged her. They are tagged on her Instagram.

I purchase all of the bath products for my daughter because of her recommendations." In her case, the allure was a mix of trust and expertise because this influencer is a nurse and mom of three and is relatable. "You literally talk to these people the way you would a friend," she added.[60]

There are several factors that are related to para-social relationships. Self-disclosure is a vital component of para-social relationships and serves to build relationships. The degree of self-disclosure from the influencer— that he or she disclosed personal aspects of their lives online—affected para-social relationship development with celebrity endorsers online.[61] Celebrities who did not disclose personal details on their social media sites were seen as lacking in honesty and authenticity. Something—even negative disclosure—is better than nothing. Negative self-disclosure can enhance para-social relationships and greater authenticity.[62] Celebrity self-disclosure online, particularly professional self-disclosure (information about work and professional lives) and personal self-disclosure (personal details), affects para-social relations.[63] Self-disclosure is an important step toward building a relationship and is also an important first step to create social presence.

Social presence is the perception associated with being psychologically involved in the interaction with the another in a mediated environment.[64] Essentially, it gets to the environment that must be present for audiences to feel a connection to the influencer online. Factors include media/technology-related factors, user factors, and social factors—all of which determine the degree of social presence. Social factors appear to be the most valuable to understanding influencer marketing. Social factors include followers' social response toward media. The importance of social factors such as informal relationships and trust,[65] humor,[66] and perceived self-disclosure[67] have been found to induce strong social presence in other types of online environments. When celebrities share and communicate aspects of their lives, followers tend to feel that celebrities were present in their lives. Social presence also facilitates more positive para-social relationships.

Another way to increase para-social relationships is to do things to maximize authenticity—which is about being perceived as representing one's true self on the screen.[68] SMIs can cultivate two types of authenticity. Passionate authenticity is maximized when SMIs can create and post content that is interesting and fits their style and identity. Transparent authenticity refers to the fact-based information about the product being endorsed and the disclosure information about the relationship between the SMI and the brand. Both are important indicators that an SMI is being authentic with followers.[69]

While much has been researched in celebrity endorsement literature and applied to SMIs, there is still much to examine. Influencer marketing is in its relative infancy as companies determine the best way to find influencers and match them with brands. Additionally, we know very little how audiences really use influencer marketing and how the influencer process really works, especially with younger audiences. We also have yet to examine some of the unintended consequences on both audiences (e.g., fear of missing out [FOMO], social comparison issues) and the influencers themselves (e.g., the difficulty of maintaining authenticity and privacy concerns). So, there is much to explore! The next chapter examines how to design effective campaigns, including goal setting and measurement, matching brands and influencers, and the best type of campaign to design for maximum effectiveness.

CHAPTER 5

Designing Influencer Marketing Campaigns

Influencers and Integrated Marketing Communications Campaigns

Oftentimes, we think of influencer marketing as a campaign (meaning a short-term effort) and as something that occurs only on a few social media platforms. Microsoft shows us that influencer marketing can be a strategic element of a larger integrated marketing campaign effort. For International Women's Day a few years ago, Microsoft used National Geographic's social media presence and some of the best-known adventure photographers to build an Instagram marketing campaign that had many other strategic elements. This effort was part of Microsoft's larger "Make What's Next" campaign in 2016 and 2017 to encourage girls to work in STEM (science, technology, engineering, and math). While the Instagram influencer campaign was key, the overall effort included other components including a 60-second TV ad, a career exploration tool created with LinkedIn, and a workshop available in Microsoft retail stores and a Facebook Live event in 2017.

The goals were to build awareness and foster positive perceptions of the brand and to create genuine messaging aimed at girls to pursue STEM education. Additionally, this allowed Microsoft to capitalize on a trending international event. A total of 30 photos taken by several popular adventure photographers were posted on five of National Geographic's Instagram channels. The photos included captions about a prominent scientist or adventurer. Influencers included Cristina Mittermeier, Ami Vitale, Krystle J Wright, and Kitra Cahana. The campaign earned 91 million views on the five accounts, 3.5 million likes, more than 115,000 likes per post, and more than 1,000 comments. For Microsoft, it worked by leveraging NatGeo's established channels and aligned them with a trusted partner as well as trusted influencers. It showcased authentic stories and imagery through sponsored posts on Instagram.[1]

Structure of Influencer Campaigns

The purpose of this chapter is to highlight ways to design an effective influencer marketing campaign. Ideally, the concept of campaign is short lived; eventually brands will consider developing deeper relationships and collaborations with a set of influencers who offer authentic content and messaging to their followers. But we must start somewhere. The chapter that follows outlines considerations for designing influencer marketing strategy. The first step examines the importance of setting goals and objectives. There are many principles around goals and objectives and understanding the consumer journey is helpful. The next step is understanding the influencers' audience and the brand's audience (known as the target market). The next issue is to examine how to best choose influencers and then how to find influencers. The following sections include campaign briefs, content creation, types of platforms, campaign structure, and performance measurement. Much of this information is based on time honored marketing strategy elements. For influencer marketing, the key "creative" decisions deal with influencer selection and message development (Figure 5.1).

Goals and Objectives

Before starting any campaign or influencer marketing program, it is best to conduct an audit of current digital assets just to establish a baseline. Amanda Russell in *The Influencer Code* recommends brands examine several areas. These include all current social media accounts (follower counts, subscribers, likes, shares, engagement ranks, and comments); website traffic; paid search results (such as click through rates (CTR) and average costs per click); e-mail marketing results (sign ups, open rates, CTR); brand sentiment from social listening tools; any instore activity for brick and mortar firms; traditional advertising metrics; SEO results; customer feedback; product reviews; and of course, financial metrics.[2] This will ensure that any additional marketing efforts—especially those involving influencers—are able to make a difference.

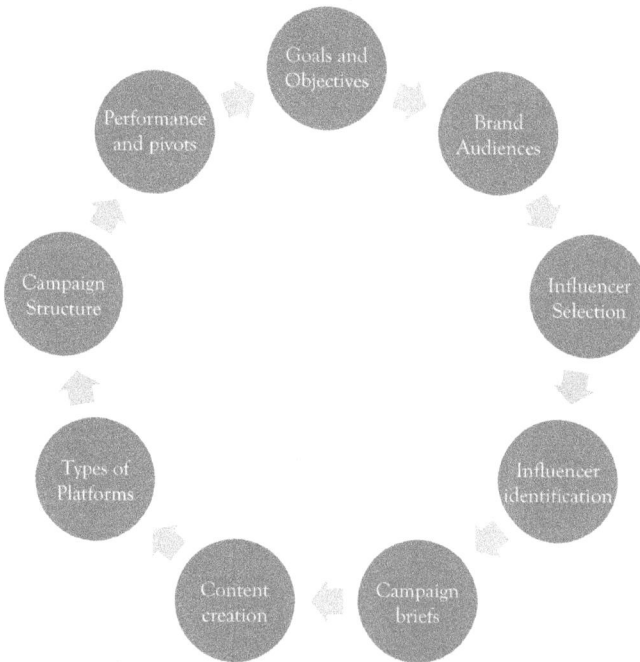

Figure 5.1 Structure of influencer campaigns

Once there is a good strategic foundation, the next step is to determine the way forward. Defining goals and objectives should be one of the first steps in designing an effective influencer marketing campaign. That said, the terms are often used interchangeably. But they are a bit different. Goals are long term and are typically the ultimate result that a brand hopes to achieve over a time period. Goals focus on the general direction for the brand. For an educational technology company, a goal could be to become a thought leader in homeschool education space. Objectives provide some structure to goals. Objectives are short and medium term and should follow the well-known S.M.A.R.T format. These are defined as follows:

- Specific: Specific objectives narrow the frame of reference.
  Example: To increase new followers by 20 percent in six months.
- Measurable: Objectives need to be quantifiable. Hard data are required and answer questions like how much or how many.
  Example: To add 100 new followers on Instagram in 45 days.

- Attainable: While optimism is great to have, objectives need to be attainable, meaning the brand must have the ability to achieve what is desired. Objectives should be based on analytics and a strong understanding of the market context.
- Relevant: Objectives should match well to the goals and be relevant to not only the industry but also the life cycle of the company (e.g., startup).
- Time oriented: A time-oriented objective includes a deadline or time parameter.

Essentially, goals are what a brand wants to achieve, and objectives provide structure on how to define success toward the goal. Let's take a company selling monogrammed bags online. The target audience for the bags are girls between 14 and 24. Before planning an influencer campaign, it is best to set goals and objectives. An effective goal for this company is to maximize growth year over year. A good objective is "to increase revenue by 10 percent by end of the fiscal year 2022." This goal is specific (revenue), measurable (10 percent), attainable (10 percent is typically not out of the question for growth targets for many industries, but that does require context), relevant (the brand is selling products), and time oriented (by end of fiscal year 2022).

For influencer marketing campaigns, there are several typical objectives that are used to measure effectiveness and return on investment (ROI). In fact, determining ROI is the most important concern among marketing managers when it comes to influencer marketing programs.[3] Key performance indicators (KPIs) are the metrics used to measure objectives. For example, if the objective is to increase brand awareness, how is it measured? Metrics include reach or impressions which can be measured online or it can be measured via website traffic through data measurement programs like Google Analytics. At this stage, it is important to align the goal, objective, and KPIs. But it is not quite that simple. It is important to think about the consumer and where they are in their purchase journey.

The Consumer Journey

Let's be honest—consumers don't usually see an ad on Facebook or see a recommendation from an influencer and immediately purchase the

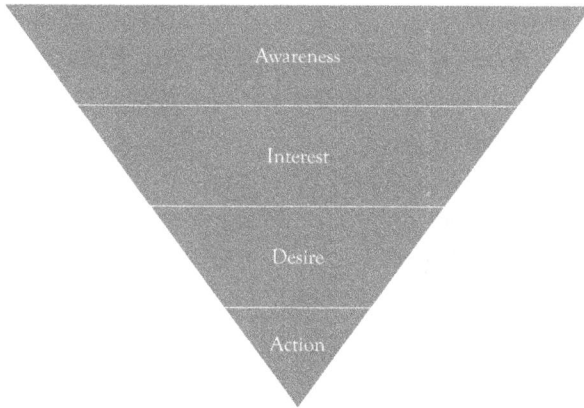

Figure 5.2 The consumer journey

product. Rather, consumers typically go through stages of a consumer journey. This concept is well known and researched in advertising and still applies in the case of influencer marketing as well. The stages of the consumer journey describe how they move from hearing about a product to buying a product and what they do after the purchase (Figure 5.2). The consumer journey includes the following:

- Awareness: Before anything gets purchased, consumers must be aware that a product even exists. Gaining awareness has been one of the primary reasons that brands invest in advertising. For influencer marketing campaigns, awareness is often seeded through content created and disseminated by influencers on social media platforms to their audiences, and awareness is one of the key objectives of influencer marketing. Typically, influencers mention a product through sponsored posts or product mentions. The message gains attention if the product or service solves a problem for the follower. It can be subtle or more overt, but the goal is to provide a solution to the problem by telling the brand's story. Attention is a huge aspect of aware-ness—that something must happen to capture the attention of consumers that then increases their awareness of product or service, and currently, audiences are paying more attention to messages from influencers than messages from brands.

- Interest/consideration: Once aware of a product, some (not all) consumers will start to do some research because either the message has piqued interest or the brand can solve a problem. The purpose of using influencers here is to build brand affinity or consideration. Influencers often provide some valuable insight to their audiences depending on the type of messaging and information being shared. This is also where other types of content marketing such as blog articles or videos become important, some of which is created by influencers and some of which is created by the brand. Additionally, consumers may examine customer reviews to get a sense for the product of interest. Here, the influencer is trying to persuade the potential customer on behalf of the brand by making more information available.

  Influencer marketing is particularly important in these first two stages. Influencers create compelling content and amplify that content on their social media platforms.

- Desire: At some point, consumers use information and recommendations to narrow down choices. The goal is to win consideration among many alternatives. Again, this is another place where other types of content marketing and native advertising can be useful to push the consumer to the next stage.

- Action: This is the point where consumers make a purchase (or not).

  Ideally, influencer marketing is about finding the right influencer and then designing the right message at the right time in a consumer's journey. Table 5.1 outlines several types of objectives that align with the consumer journey as well as KPIs that connect to the objective.

So, at the start, it is easy to see that having a good foundation on where to go and how to measure success is important. This sets up many other decisions—from how to choose the influencer to how to choose the platform and message. But first, we must understand audiences— the brand's audience and eventually the influencer's audience to ensure a match.

Table 5.1 *Types of objectives and KPIs*

Consumer decision funnel	Objectives	KPI[4]
Awareness	Brand awareness Reach new audiences Amplify reach and engagement	Reach; website traffic; views; CTR; engagement rate; share of voice; impressions
Interest (or consideration)	Audience interest Engagement building Word of mouth/buzz Alignment with the brand Attitude and perceptions Follower growth	Engagement; shares; quality of influencer content; audience sentiment; clicks; comments
Desire (or preference)	Audience interest Share of voice relative to competitors Drive lead generation Growing community	Engagement; shares; quality of influencer content; audience sentiment; comments; conversions (not sales)
Action	Generate sales	Links through social commerce; sales; average order value; conversion metrics
Satisfaction (loyalty)	Brand advocacy and loyalty Manage reputation and customer satisfaction	New followers; organic mentions Net promoter score

Brand and Influencer Audiences

Interestingly, Brian Solis argues that the future of influence is "more significant than a legacy-based marketing program that emulates celebrity endorsements or advocacy programs in new paradigms." He believes that empathy and customer centricity are the keys to taking influence to the next level.[5] To truly understanding the audience (brand or influencer), it is critical to think about the people who are in the community—why they belong—as more than just numbers. The influencer communities are closely tied together—to the influencer and to each other. As such, it requires a more human approach than traditional marketing. The brand needs to understand what the community needs and values. Relationships should really drive this process since marketers are borrowing social capital from influencers to sell products to their communities.[6]

When putting it into marketing terms, the "target market" is the group of people who may/will buy a product or service. Traditionally, marketers defined target audiences in terms of demographics (e.g., age, gender, and income) and typically cast a wide net. That worked for a while. But now, audience size is only one component. In fact, if an audience is small, it can still be quite profitable for products and services if they are solving a consumer problem. For example, if Osaka's field hockey stick is trying to identify a market, it may be small (e.g., people who play field hockey, mostly girls between the ages of 6 and 24 who live in the northeast and Midwest United States and who have access to a club, school, or field to play field hockey). But that group is passionate with specific needs, so if Osaka can offer a great product, then Osaka can be profitable. So, it is important to try to narrow the audience and design the message to them as opposed to trying to appeal to a large audience.

Of course, demographics are useful. However, they only get a brand so far. Psychographics tap into attitudes, character, values, interests and hobbies, and lifestyles of consumers. This helps understand the "why" behind consumer behavior. Shopping behavior taps into how a consumer shops (online, in store), feels about pricing (prestige, bargain) and what need or desire the consumer was trying to satisfy. Additionally, it can be important to understand how the audience engages with social media. The 90-9-1 rule basically states that 90 percent of users on a social media platform simply consume content. Nine percent occasionally engage with content which constitutes the community. Then, 1 percent represents who creates and disseminates most of the content. It is important to know the social media makeup of the audience to better target messaging and campaigns. In order to craft clarity around these data, marketers can create consumer journey maps based on audience information.

A good way to put this information together is by developing a buyer persona. It is a fictitious representation of the consumer based on research and data collected about the target market. It is a narrative—based on demographics, psychographics, pain points, and challenges as well as delights. Essentially, this is a great way to understand the problem that a consumer is trying to solve. At the end of the chapter, take a look at examples for a persona and consumer journey map.

Choosing Influencers

Choosing influencers is one of the most important decisions (and the toughest) that brands need to make when developing an influencer campaign. The "pillars of influence" was first developed by Brian Solis and then expanded by Scott Guthrie of Ketchum London.[7] Amanda Russell argues that five principles—reach, recognition, reference, relevance, and resonance—are important to understanding influence and any influencer should be assessed against them. Reach is defined as the overall size of the influencer's following across all platforms. Recognition is defined as how recognizable the influencer is for the audience of interest. Reference is defined as who else in the category is paying attention to the influencer's work. Relevance is defined as the degree that the influencer is associated with a topic (e.g., expertise in a particular category). And resonance is defined as how well the influencer can engage with the audience. It is also known as the engagement rate.

Given that true influence takes time, the term "campaign" may not even be as relevant for some brands. A top trend going into 2021 is that rather than single transactional collaborations, brands should develop deeper and more meaningful partnerships with influencers. This sentiment was heard from a variety of brands during AdWeek's Social Media Week LA conference in June 2021. There are multiple reasons for this shift. First, if the ultimate goal is sales (and most often it is), making a sale takes some time. Even influencers with highly engaged audiences only have so much control over action (even influencers who have taught their audience to purchase). As such, it is tough for any influencer to make a significant long-term contribution in a single sponsored post.[8] Relationships are the key here. In fact, Brian Solis talks about the importance of relationships and longer-term collaborations with influencers. Chief Marketing Officer at Brand Innovators, Ted Rubin, says "A return on relationships is the value that is accrued by a person or brand due to nurturing a relationship over time. This will demonstrate that the influencer is true to the brand, and this true relationship connection will pass through to the customer."[9] Trust-based relationships do take time and effort to sustain over time. And it is important for both parties. "If I can give brands value and I can teach influencers how to recognize their value and capitalize on what their true value is, then everyone walks away from a partnership happy and feeling like they got what they wanted out if it," said Lynsey Eaton, CEO and founder of Estate Five, who manages macro-influencers and connects them with select client brands.

Michael Haenlein and his colleagues outline four issues to consider when choosing influencers. First, it is important to consider how influencers are categorized. Chapter 3 discussed this in some detail, with the caveat that the number of followers is only one metric to consider (and not always the most important metric). Rather it is also important to consider the audience composition and engagement rate as well. Second, they argue it is important to consider influencers as professionals and creators and realize the time and effort they have spent to build their audiences (and in some cases, their businesses). Third, choose influencers who are already influential in their social circle and choose those who have passion and authenticity. Last, consider multiple platforms and connect these to other traditional advertising efforts as well as offline efforts.[10] So let's examine some considerations in more detail, knowing that there is not "one" way to do this.

Looking for Influencers

1. Be sure to set your criteria. Check out issues like engagement rate, audience relevancy, content quality, location, topics, any special skills like language or athletics, and brand tone. There are many criteria to consider here.
2. Make a list. Using a variety of methods discussed later, make a good list and evaluate influencers based on criteria. It is also good to rate them on a scale of 1 to 5 and that can help winnow it down.
3. Select your influencers. Be sure to validate the size and reputation of the audiences for your influencers. Make the deal! (More on that in Chapter 6).[11]

There are several considerations for choosing an influencer. These include a variety of influencer metrics, where consumers are in the consumer journey and a few other considerations.

Influencer Metrics

The easiest way (and up to this point, the way most brands selected influencers) is based on the number of followers. Chapter 3 outlines the various tiers of influencers based on that metric. And for some campaigns, choosing celebrity or macro-influencers perhaps makes sense to maximize reach and awareness. For others, especially for local campaigns, it makes sense to focus on influencers with smaller follower numbers. Instead of relying only on follower counts, there are other metrics to consider. These include the following:

- Reach: Discussed earlier, the number of followers can be used to determine an influencer. It is important to dig a little deeper into the numbers to ensure that there are no fake followers (discussed in Chapter 6). The purpose of maximizing reach is similar to a large media buy—how to get as many "eyeballs" as possible.
- Average engagement rate: This metric is measured by the number of likes and comments divided by the number of followers. It attempts to assess how excited the audience is about the influencer and the content that the influencer posts. Studies have shown that influencers with smaller audiences typically have a higher engagement rate, and brands are starting to focus on that more than reach.
- Audience quality: Related to engagement, this examines how the audience is engaged across a variety of content and the nuances in how they respond to various content. For example, do audience member respond in passive (likes) or more active (comments and shares) ways?
- Audience relevancy and composition: It is vital that the influencer's audience are potential buyers for a brand's product or service. This includes demographics and psychographics for the audience. Brands are looking for a match between the influencer's audience the potential target market for the product or service.

- Exclusivity issues: Some brands may want the influencer to only represent their products and services. For some categories, that makes sense. However, in other categories— beauty and fashion, for example—this may not make as much sense because people typically mix up brands. Additionally, exclusivity is relevant after the influencer, and the brand has built a long-term, mutually beneficial relationship.
- Influencer background: This includes the expertise of the influencer, the level of talent for content development, and how the audience connects with that content. This also includes perceptions of authenticity, which has been shown to be a crucial element to success.
- Budget: Sometimes selection comes down to the brand's budget and whether the influencer's price to post is in line with it. The price per post will depend on a variety of factors.
- Brand alignment: This includes whether a brand and influencer align in terms of image and price point. "If I am Neiman Marcus and I'm looking at an influencer who has a conversion price that is traditionally in the $400 to $500 range, that probably can work well," said Lynsey Eaton CEO and cofounder of Estate Five. "But if she is a mom sitting at home with spit up on her shirt, that probably won't align well."
- Campaign KPIs: One way to choose influencers is to consider influencers who are good at converting on key campaign performance indicators. For example, some influencers are great for sales; others are better for alignment. Eaton argues that this is the best way to go. "What the mistake that brands make is that essentially they will come in and they will want a certain woman with 700,000 followers and they want them to sell this much product, but that influencer has not trained her audience into action," she says. "Audiences follow influencers for different reasons. If sales is the goal, we have a woman with 180,000 followers who has trained her audience to purchase. They listen to her. My first question is *always* what is the KPI?"[12]

Consumer Journey

One way to examine how to choose influencers is to consider the consumer journey and the objectives related to the funnel (see Table 5.1). For example, the top of the funnel is about gaining awareness. If the brand is large enough, it can make sense to use macro-influencers or even celebrity influencers. The reason? Reach. Influencers with that many followers can reach millions of people. It is expensive to engage them but can be effective at creating top of mind awareness. When moving to interest or consideration, mass market brands can continue to use macro-influencers but can also consider micro-influencers, and many brands are moving toward influencers with smaller audiences and higher engagement. The goal here is connect with the audience in a deeper way. If the goal is to maximize evaluation and action (e.g., purchase), micro-influencers and nano-influencers have higher engagement levels because their followers trust them. They are perceived as authentic and are typically seen as more expert in the product category.

Other Considerations

There are several other considerations when determining how to include as a potential influencer. Andrea Arias, associate brand manager for Cetaphil, said that she likes to look at trends. She likes to identify up and coming influencers by looking at data that show influencer growth in terms of followers and engagement levels over time.[13] Brittany Knight, lifestyle brand manager for Nike, said that for some initiatives, they look for something specific. Knight works with influencers in Los Angeles. She focuses on engaging young Black and Latinx women. "We look at Dubsmash which is similar to TikTok but has probably 90 percent Black girls," said Knight. "We are looking at engagement and influence and are looking at more of a long-term relationship."[14] As such, there are a variety of considerations. "I am seeing more and more that brands want to work with a really specific type of person that has a really specific message to a really specific group of people. And I think this shows a shift and the way that brands are understanding the value of influencers," said Addi McCauley of IZEA.

Overall, when selecting an influencer, brands do need to compromise. "In influencer marketing, I feel that there's awareness, there's alignment and there's engagement. Pick one or two but you can't get all three," said Lynsey Eaton of Estate Five.

Perspective From an Influencer

Remember that the best influencer marketing campaigns represent a partnership—between the brand and the influencer. So it is also important to consider what is important to influencers when determining who to work with. West Gissinger is a Dallas-based fitness influencer and Pilates instructor who is a brand ambassador for Outdoor Voices and Carbon38. I talked to West about how she connects with brands. "Most often for me, a brand will reach out to me directly via DM or e-mail. If I feel the partnership is a good fit and aligned with my everyday lifestyle, we discuss the logistics of the collaboration," she said. "My favorite collaborations are with brands and people I have met personally through using their products and services. I have an ongoing collaboration with my hairdresser and I met her through being a client of mine!" Gissinger emphasized the importance of fit between her lifestyle and the brand. "I always ask myself—would I actually use this or buy this—and if the answer is no, then it is no to the collaboration for me. I turn down a majority of collaboration opportunities that come my way for that reason. I am not one to post about something just because they are paying me to giving me a free product. I really have to believe in it," she added. "People are smart. They can read right through an inauthentic post. And maintaining authenticity is super important to me."

Gissinger mentioned her work as a brand ambassador. To her this means acting as an "arm of the company" that helps build community in addition to brand awareness. "In my experience, you are given more insight into the happenings and initiatives of the brand. The brand also invests in you," she said. "Both Carbon38 and Outdoor Voices do a great job of supporting fitness professionals in their industry. Being a brand ambassador allows me to connect and collaborate with a like-minded group of people."[15]

Influencer Identification

This is a tough issue since there are so many potential influencers out there. There are databases that scrape website content based on filters and keywords that can assist marketers to find, research, and track influencers across several social media platforms. Popular databases include BuzzSumo and NinjaOutreach among others. Additionally, marketers can conduct a manual search that includes an influencer's social media platforms, associations and groups, blogs, video blogs, forums and communities, and traditional media. While this can be tedious, it is important to assure brand safety.[16] Influencer marketing agencies can also help identify potential influencers (some of which they have a relationship with and others that they don't). Agencies will act as an intermediary when developing the campaign. Influencer marketplaces are two-sided platform to connect brands and influencers. Essentially influencers opt-in to a marketplace and marketers can then search the marketplace for the campaign needs. Additionally, the marketplace often facilitates the relationship around communication and payment, which then saves time and money for both brands and influencers. Many influencers belong to multiple marketplaces. Last, some brands want to cultivate the relationship in house. Pepsi's Rockstar Energy (discussed in earlier chapters) made a conscious effort to build deeper relationships between influencers and the brand team, arguing the need for the brand to have a face.

Sometimes you must get creative. "We had a campaign for a company that was really wanting to work with moms as they gave birth and started their breastfeeding journey. They wanted to follow moms for the first 21 days because their research showed that if a mom can make it through the first 21 days of breastfeeding, she would probably stick with it for the first few months," said Addi McCauley of IZEA. The issue was then how to identify those influencers. IZEA looked through content where women were showing their bump pictures and talking about how many weeks pregnant they were. "We were literally looking at people posting pregnancy announcements and early first trimester posts or second trimester posts so that we had enough lead time to identify the right fit for the campaign."

Campaign Briefs

Whenever working with an influencer, it is important to develop a communication or campaign brief, just like any other marketing effort. The brief includes basic information such as brand overview, campaign objectives, messaging, audience overview, content deliverables and timelines, review process, performance metrics, and payment. This will help influencers to create the content that will resonate the best with audiences. The biggest difference with influencer marketing is the degree of control that the brand should exhibit over the content and messaging. When a brand tries to have tight control, there can be several misfires. First, it reduces creative freedom for the influencer. When there are multiple influencers, reducing creative freedom can result in content that is too similar and not interesting and as such, will not resonate. Second, some influencers will refuse to work with a brand because reducing creative freedom also tends to reduce authenticity, and influencers are just as worried about their own brand safety as the brands paying for the content. It is better to provide guidelines that can result in authentic and quality content that deliver results.[17] AT&T TV decided to give creative freedom to their influencers in the TikTok house The Crib Around the Corner, which is the first Black TikTok house. It consists of five Black creators who live in the house for six months and create content for AT&T TT who is the brand sponsor. Instead of tight campaign briefs, the creators were given a simple message and they were allowed to improve and do the rest. They argue it is best to treat the creator has collaborators and not puppets. "Trust in humans and keep experimenting," said Nick Bianchi, director of digital and social media for AT&T during Adweek's Social Media Week LA.[18]

Types of Social Media Platforms

Social media platforms are the connective tissue of the influencer marketing ecosystem. These platforms are where influencers build their audiences. They are linked—the influencers need the platforms for exposure to their audience and platforms need the content created by people—including influencers. That said, not all social media platforms are created equally

Petfluencers

What if the influencer is not even human? What if the influencer is a pet? Well, there is big money in being a pet influencer and brands are starting to take notice. The Westminster Kennel Club (WKC) founded in 1877 began promoting its 2020 Best of Show on TikTok. It featured videos from leading pet influencers—like Loki the golden retriever—to hype the event. The video from Loki received close to three million views! Interestingly, the top pet influencers earn a lot of money. "On average, someone with 10,000 followers is getting around $1–2K per post; someone with 500,000 followers earns around $5K per post and someone with more than 1 million followers is in the $10K range," said Loni Edwards, CEO of the Dog Agency which represents the highest earning pet influencers. Dog Agency connects brands—like Bush's Baked Beans—with dogs and cats. And pets can convert! According to research from Collective Bias, people are 10 percent more likely to buy goods endorsed by a famous pet versus just 3 percent from a human influencer. The number one pet influencer is Jiffpom, the Pomeranian pup with nearly 10 million followers on Instagram who regularly earns an average of $32,045 per endorsement. Nala Cat with more than 4.3 million followers earns $14,253 per post. We are living in an influencer economy for everyone![19]

when it comes to influencer marketing. Michael Haenlein and his colleagues argued in an article in the *California Management Review* that Facebook, YouTube, Instagram, Twitter, and TikTok are the most important social media platforms. Yes, Twitch (for gamers) and Snapchat are important too, but they felt that these five represented the most significant platforms right now. In a survey of enterprise marketers (more than $1 billion+ revenue), marketers felt that influencer marketing is no longer a one-off tactic but rather a sophisticated part of the marketing mix. Budget and commitment levels are increasing. Instagram is still the platform of choice with more than 93 percent stating they play to use it in 2021. Relatedly, Instagram stories will be part of the campaign plan for 83 percent and 37 percent of marketers are planning to experiment with Instagram's Reels. TikTok saw the largest increase with 68 percent of marketers saying they will use it. From there, the list of social platforms include Facebook (68 percent), YouTube (48 percent), Pinterest (35 percent), Snapchat (26 percent), Twitter (32 percent), Blogs (25 percent), and Twitch (13 percent).[20]

Regardless of which platform a brand chooses, it is important to understand what about the platform makes it most useful for influencer marketing and that each platform has its identity. Each platform has its culture, language, and styles that have been adapted by the influencers on that platform. Remember, most influencers have a primary platform where they are most popular. Content in one platform cannot be easily transferred to other platforms (although there are ways to repurpose content and brands can and should do that for their traditional advertising efforts). Brands should ensure that they engage with influencers with deep experience on the social media platform.[21]

More detail is provided on three platforms used for most influencer marketing—Instagram, TikTok, and YouTube. Table 5.2 includes larger

Table 5.2 Social media platforms

Platform	Focus	Influencer interest	Uses
Instagram (Gen Y, Z)	Image and video (stories, reels)	Top influencer platform	Entertainment, follow friends, follow brands
TikTok (Gen Y, Z)	Video	Top influencer platform	Entertainment, follow friends
YouTube (Gen X, Y, Z)	Video	Top influencer platform	Follow brands, entertainment, news
Facebook (Gen Y, X, Boomers)	Text Image Video		Keep in contact with family and friends, news, entertainment
Snapchat (Gen Y, Z)	Disappearing photos and videos		Keep in contact with family and friends, entertainment
Twitter (Gen Y, X)	Text		Keep in contact with family and friends, news, entertainment
Pinterest (Gen Y, X)	Photos and images		Entertainment, inspiration
Twitch (Gen Y, Z)	Live streaming		Entertainment— gaming specific
Clubhouse TBD	Audio only		TBD

set of social media platforms. Let's take a look at some of the platforms and what makes them great candidates for influencer marketing.

Instagram

Instagram is currently the most popular social media platform for influencer marketing. By the end of 2020, there are more than 130 million U.S. users and 67 percent of U.S. adults are on the platform. That said, 89 percent of Instagram users are outside of the United States. Instagram is popular with Generation Z and millennials—in fact, 72 percent of teens are on Instagram. It is also popular with businesses. More than 75 percent of businesses use Instagram in some way.[22] The photo and video-based app is known for its aesthetically pleasing grid and the ability to curate content. It primarily shows the content of users that people relate to—for example, following. In the past few years, Instagram added Instagram Stories (like Snapchat stories), IGTV (for longer form video content), and Reels which allows for a new way to create and discover short entertaining videos. The app offers the perfect space for influencers to authentically recommend products and services to their loyal audience members. The pool of influencers is vast and includes several categories—from health and beauty to DIY and sports. Brands pay influencers to develop and disseminate sponsored posts in a way that connects with their followers, and the price of the post is based on the number of followers and engagement rate. Engagement on Instagram is high (one study shows 29.67 percent engagement rate).[23] Campaign types include sponsored posts, contests, branded content, and reviews via product mentions. Instagram is a staple of influencer marketing and at this point should be considered in most brand campaigns.

Olay set out to stand out in the crowded beauty space. The legacy brand elected to leverage Instagram influencer marketing and cause marketing. The campaign centered on several female influencers to encourage women to be "unapologetically" themselves and disregard comments about being "too much." Olay branded the campaign for the Fearless9 and built a microsite that hosted behind the scenes footage of a Vogue photoshoot. The purpose of the campaign centered around inspiring messaging. Olay wanted to connect to diverse audiences to

generate relatability using female influencers; to increase brand awareness around defying societal expectations; and to establish brand affinity and sales. Influencers included models and athletes as well as other
"powerhouses" using the #faceanything hashtag. The campaign was a
28-day challenge to break free of normal beauty campaigns. Social reach
included 298K video views and 21K followers targeted. Engagement
rate was 8.33 percent through 1.4 million likes, 11,000 comments,
and more than 1,000 hashtag uses. Why did it work? Olay chose a
core group of influencers of a variety of types and then supported the
influencers to share personal stories and then connected with audiences
through authentic messages.[24]

TikTok

In 2016, the Chinese-based ByteDance launched TikTok which has
become Generation Z's most coveted app after merging with the lip sync-
ing video app, Music.ly. In 2020, it became the most downloaded app
in the world with 700 million active users and an expected 1.2 billion in
2021. It is also the fastest growing social media platform with 80 million
active users in the United States. Users spend an overage 52 minutes daily
on TikTok and 32.5 percent of users are ages 10 to 19 and 29.5 percent
are ages 20 to 29, with females outnumbering males almost 2:1 in the
United States. TikTok also has the highest average engagement per post
(17.5 percent) which is key for brand managers.[25]

Why? What makes TikTok so popular? Four design issues make
TikTok useful for audiences. First, the "for you" algorithm is a recommendation engine that directs users to relevant content based on their
browsing habits. This changes over time as the browsing habits change.
This ensures authentic content. Second, TikTok contains captivating
short-form entertainment that does not take itself too seriously. It is
fun—not curated and perfect. The content is approachable making it
popular with users. Third, there is a native scrolling format since the app
is built to scroll from video to video ensuring users don't have to work too
hard to discover new content. Last, TikTok provides accessible creator
tools for everyone to become a creator which supports the quick and easy
production of user-generated content.[26]

Given TikTok's massive growth and global viewership, brands are heading to the social platform. Brands are considering more TikTok creators over Instagram, partially for the chance for content to go viral. In terms of marketing spend, brands are trying out things in TikTok. Over the last quarter, "there's been a significant acceleration in the investments our brands are making on TikTok," noted Brendan Gahan, chief social officer and partner at Mekanism. "It's shocking how quickly they've managed to go from that experimental bucket to nearly being a campaign staple on par with Facebook. TikTok is not there yet, but you can see it trending that way."[27] Brands like Chobani, Verizon, and Alaska Airlines have prioritized TikTok influencers in their marketing efforts. Currently, most campaigns are designed to drive brand awareness, and more brands are seeing TikTok as part a staple of social media spending as opposed to a test and learn.[28]

TikTok has several branding opportunities, including using influencers, and has built a tool for third parties to easily discover influences on the platform. TikTok allows brands to partner with creators to produce content for branding initiatives. Other options on TikTok include the hashtag challenge, paid social advertising, and of course, brand profiles.

Sony Home Pictures Entertainment collaborated with several TikTok creators to promote the movie Jumanji: The Next Level. They partnered with Zach King (one of the most popular TikTok influencers), New Rockstars, and SuperHeroKids to create dedicated videos for TikTok, YouTube, and Instagram. Engagement rate on TikTok was 16.2 percent (higher than the other platforms), and Zach King received 19.8 million views on his TikTok video. This managed to garner a social reach of 67.8 million and 25.3 million total views.[29]

YouTube

Content marketing trends indicate that video is more important than other types of content. YouTube remains an important to tool for authentic storytelling and provides an avenue for longer form content. In fact, YouTube was the place where many SMIs got their start especially in fashion, beauty, and gaming. There has been an uptick in content related to all other types of subjects—from fitness to finance to travel. Currently, there are 1.78 billion global views for YouTube with an expected increase to 1.87 billion in 2021. More than 92 percent of the audience claims they use it weekly. The highest earning influencer on YouTube in 2020 was Ryan's ToyShow where 9-year-old Ryan Kaji reviews toys. He earned $29.5 million in 2020. YouTube is a favorite platform for 53 percent of Gen Z males and 42 percent of Gen Z females.[30] There are several types of ways to use YouTube on influencer channels, including unboxing videos, haul videos, how to videos, behind the scenes videos, comedy sketches, morning routines, and day in the life vlogs. Several brands have used these types of video content successful, especially beauty, fashion, and fitness.

Other Social Media Platforms

While the ones above are currently seeing the most influencer marketing action, that is not to say these are the only ones. But there have been changes. Facebook is still the largest social media platform (in terms of active users, monthly sessions, and weekly posters), but the audience has skewed older over the past few years. Users tend to be in their 40s for Facebook. Additionally, engagement rates have declined, and more people have left Facebook than some of the other platforms. Few Generation Z are Facebook users, highlighting the changing media consumption patterns based on age. Twitter is text-based making influencer marketing a bit more difficult. The same can be said for LinkedIn, which has a more specific, work-related focus. Snapchat is very popular with Generation Z, but the messages do disappear and are not sharable, making it harder to develop content for brands. Twitch is an amazing platform for livestreaming for the gaming industry and has a variety of users and influencers. But the focus is still limited. Clubhouse, the audio only social media platform, is the newest to the ecosystem, so the verdict is still out on how it will be used. Blogs and podcasts are still utilized for specific reasons. Podcasts have seen a huge surge in popularity. Oftentimes, however, people with influential blogs or podcasts have other social media platforms they use to connect to audiences.[31]

Campaign Structures and Beyond

There are several general ways to use influencer marketing campaigns. Some of the "structure" depends on the social media platform. But some campaign structures platform agnostic. Regardless, most campaigns are centered around content—both creating it, cocreating it, amplifying, and distributing it.

Content creation is one of the most valuable aspects of working with influencers. According to Neal Shaffer,[32] there are several aspects of content creation. First, brands are now considering outsourcing their content creation and acknowledging the true talent of influencers as photographers, videographers, editors, and writers. They utilize influencer's skills. Second, brands can sometimes cocreate content with influencers, thus establishing a partnership. There are several types of content that can be used as part of an influencer marketing campaign beyond sponsored posts. These include lists (think about top 10 things to do in San Diego), infographics, how to articles (very useful for several categories like beauty and fashion), what posts (posts that start with "what" like ... what to do), why posts (articles that attempt to answer why), videos, live feeds, live feed takeovers, webinars, podcasts, and so many others.[33] Remember that many of these need a call to action to direct audiences toward the expected behavior. This is really a place where influencer marketing and content marketing intersect. Third, there is the value of visual storytelling and visual voice. Shaffer also argues that since these new types of visual communication tools have popped up, brands have struggled to align their imagery and find their visual voice and learn how to communicate that voice on social media. As a quick example, beauty companies like Sephora, Nordstrom, and Target have done a good job of refining their visual voice on Instagram. All use influencers to assist.[34]

The other value of creator content is the cost. "I know coming from the brand side, that on the agency side the production costs continue to skyrocket and are not stopping," said Ryan Schram, COO of IZEA. "At the same time, tools get better and in the hands of ordinary people and the work that they are creating oftentimes look as good if not better than the million dollar shoot I just got done." He added, "You know you had foodies who had better lenses and better videography tools than some of the pros and they also were doing it themselves. They were coming up with the idea, the recipe, the shoot. And all of a sudden, you start thinking to yourself that it is the ability to hit social reach and the ability to touch all these platforms and the brand gets a license to use that content and repurpose it." In many cases, the content created—for example, a video—can be sliced up and become preroll for a brand across programmatic advertising buys or can be used in store. There are so many possibilities.

Influencers also amplify and distribute content. This is where the paid component of influencer marketing comes into play and where it intersects with native advertising. This is also called sponsored content distribution and is often identified as #sponsoredcontent and #ad. Approaches include sponsored Facebook updates, follow a brand, sponsored tweets, videos, photos, blog post, e-mail, twitter follower, livestream, and pin. Brands can get experimental. Clorox has been a leader in influencer marketing but raised their profile with a mysterious artist known as CLRX, who attracted fans on social media with a debut song "So Clean." Her songs were on Apple Music and SoundCloud promoted on Instagram and Twitter and even a website. CLRX also earned more than 135,000 views on YouTube and has offers from multiple record labels. But she is not an up-and-coming artist but rather than a partnership between Clorox and Brand Synergy Group. "'So Clean' is about cleaning up life, both emotionally and physically," said Magnus Jonsson, global vice president of brand engagement and U.S. vice president of cleaning at The Clorox Company. "The strategy behind CLRX is to appeal to young adults in an authentic, nonintrusive manner that's more about communicating with them than at them."[35]

There are several ways to work with influencers as well. Most are financially compensated—mostly as a monetary transaction—but that is not always the case. Especially for nano-influencers, other compensation options include giving them products hoping that they will mention it (note: it is important to adhere to FTC guidelines discussed in Chapter 6). A giveaway or sweepstakes is another way to collaborate with influencers. It is a combination of giving away and gifting for influencer review. If the brand's product is too expensive to give away, sometimes affiliate marketing can be used. Influencers can become an affiliate marketer for the brand, and as a result, they can get some compensation based on each purchase. This has the added advantage of tracking sales in a pretty easy way. Amazon Influencer Shops is an attractive option through their platform. Promotion and discounts can also be used for tracking where influencers use a tracking code that is used as a discount at checkout for their followers.[36]

In addition to campaigns, brands can use influencers in many ways. Remember, influencers are people—they are advocates for the brand. Connecting them to additional aspects of the overall business can make a lot of sense. First, brands can use influencers to help identify target audiences. Influencers know their followers—their needs, wants, and desires—and this is insightful data for brands. They bring a different level of depth of the audience. Second, brands can use influencers to assist with product design and redesign. Using the insight that influencers have about potential markets, this too is useful information for brands. They can suggest improvements and assist in product redesign. And many influencers would jump at the chance to have cocreator partnerships where brands and influencers launch a cobranded product or collection where the influencer has co-ownership. Nike has done this for years—think about the Michael Jordan basketball shoe and how successful it has been for decades! Interestingly, according to Neal Shaffer, five of the top female clothing brands in China were started by Chinese influencers. Third, influencers can help brands hone marketing messages ensuring that it is tapping into the needs and desires of the audience. Influencers know the language, culture, and memes—the ways that a brand can appeal to audiences. Last, one of the best things that influencers do is create content, much of which can be repurposed for other aspects of the advertising and marketing campaign.[37]

Performance and Pivots

During any influencer marketing campaign, it is important to continue to measure success (or lack thereof). In some cases, the cause of failure has to do with a lack of access to data and metrics. It is the lack of analysis and critical thinking about the short-term and long-term impact of campaigns and partnerships. Campaigns should review both short-term and long-term metrics. One of the criticisms of influencer marketing (and in fact, digital marketing overall) is the focus on vanity metrics. Vanity metrics are measurements of likes, follower counts, comments, and so forth. These focus on short-term results and do provide some directional impact. These metrics have a place but should be the starting point as opposed to the ending point of measurement. True influence and the value of the relationship are more sophisticated than that.

Amanda Russell sets out some great ideas on performance measurement in her book.[38] In order to really understand performance and then determine what types of pivots are needed, it is vital to review the goals and objectives set forth at the beginning. What was the purpose of the campaign and how did the brand view success? Importantly, review the baseline information. This will ensure that the goals and objectives (and metrics) are going to make an impact. Second, determine how to track the progress. Most will be strictly quantitative but will yield useful data. A few options:

- Coupon codes that are provided to each influencer to track sales.
- Tags and hashtags track mentions and references to the brand and topics.
- Tracking pixels will allow brands to see website visits and can identify the social platforms that are performing well.
- Social listening and alerts set up to track brand mentions online.
- Affiliate links are like coupon codes and are simple ways to tie influencer content to results.
- Dedicated landing pages are specific pages created on the website that influencers can direct audiences to that can include special editions or products.
- Instagram's in-app purchasing allows users to directly purchase items from the platform.
- Google analytics and other measurement programs should be used at a minimum to provide basic details on how people use the website.

Now that the brand has the data in hand, it may become apparent that pivots or revisions need to be implemented. That is one of the best things about digital and social media marketing—the ability to make quick changes. Remain in contact with the influencer to ensure that changes can be implemented quickly. This is especially important as the relationship between the brand and the influencer grows.

Brands are concerned with better ways to measure performance. Earned media value (EMV) is a PR-based metric used to measure earned media. Essentially it assigns a dollar value to the various actions associated with content. EMV considers reach or actions such as comments or likes and the amount normally paid for CPM (or the cost to reach one thousand people). Recently, Trybe Dynamics determined that EMV could be another way to look at influencer marketing and focus on the earned part of the equation—that there is a misconception around influencer marketing being all pay to play and pointed to Wet + Wild cosmetics who had more than 6,000 creators develop more than 7,000 pieces of content on their own. That said they can use EMV to identify campaign successes. Tula Skincare saw a 32 percent increase in EMV boosting its EMV to $28 million during its recent "return to normal" campaign.[39] Google is also starting to review performance through a different lens as well. Google argues moving past EMV to measuring brand lift. This was done in order to get closer to attribution since that is a true way to measure impact. Google has been able to conduct brand surveys using YouTube's Brand Connect to track various aspects of brand lift and then compare it to other tactics like television. Interestingly, they have seen a brand lift using influencers, which is close to the scale of television.[40]

Designing effective campaigns is hard but can make a huge impact for the ability of influencer marketing to build impactful brands. The issue with influencer marketing is how quickly things change and how large a role that technology will inevitably play. But the beauty of this is that the brand can get a better idea of its ROI. Measuring ROI comes down to three issues: What was your objective, did you achieve it, and at what cost? Then, influencer marketing can be compared to other tactics.

The Anatomy of an Influencer Campaign

A great way to understand this is through an example. Truly Good[41] is a health restaurant based in Dallas, Texas, started in 2019 by two friends who met at culinary school. They opened a small, hip and upscale restaurant located in the uptown area in Dallas. This is one of the wealthiest and youngest areas in the city. They offer a full line of lunch and dinner options, which include several vegan and vegetarian options as well as a new line of protein bowls. They also offer several lines of wine and beer that is healthy with fewer calories than the other options. Truly Good has a great patio with a fountain, busy happy hour, and a well-trained and friendly staff. While they have relied on WOM and some social media to increase awareness, the owners—Kate and Carol—feel that it is time to increase their marketing presence. But they don't have a major budget and—at least right now—they are limited to one location in Dallas. So, they set a few objectives:

First, they want to *increase the sales of their protein bowls by 20 percent in the next three months*. Second, they want to *increase the awareness and the reservations for a new Saturday brunch offering. They believe having 10 reservations on average for the first month would be considered a success*. Note that both are SMART objectives, allowing Kate and Carol to be able to measure their success. To really understand, it is important to review their baseline snapshot. In this case, here is a quick overview:

- Truly Good averages 20 to 30 lunch customers during the week and 40 to 50 dinner customers during the week. It increases during the weekend (especially on Sundays) but the Saturday lunch averages are lower.
- Truly Good has an Instagram account (4,500 followers), Facebook page (972 followers), and blog where they post. They post one to two times per week on Instagram (average 6–10 comments depending on the post), weekly on Facebook, and biweekly blog posts (no comments). They also have a general website and have reviews on Yelp and Google. Most of the comments and evaluations are positive around their service and food quality. They have been written up in a few local Dallas publications over the past year.

Second, it is important to understand Truly Good's customers. Most of their core customers are women aged 20 to 30 who work and live in the area. They visit Truly Good three times per month, often with friends. To understand customers, a persona and journey map can be useful. Take a look at these two useful tools (Figures 5.3 and Table 5.3).

Jen, Jess, and Brenna

About: Three friends who have known each other for 5 years (all college friends); ages 24 and 25; work in banking, fashion and advertising; health interests (yoga, cycling, running); Jess is vegan

Attitudes: Optimistic, fun, ambitious but not over the top, love great food, wine and atmosphere

Goals: Looking for a great place to connect on Saturdays after their morning workouts; love healthy and light food.

Pain points: Not enough healthy food options and they feel there is a lack of places that are interesting and pretty. Also they want a good place that is good for Instagram worthy posts!

Figure 5.3 Persona

Table 5.3 Customer journey map

Stage of the Process or User Journey	Stage 1 Friday weekend plans	Stage 2 Saturday morning workouts	Stage 3 Eat	Stage 4 After brunch
User Activities	The three friends are texting plans for the weekend. It includes work, workout, social	Girls head to morning workout classes starting at 8am. It is a long workout day.	Decide where to meet for brunch. Want somewhere fun & casual with great food	Happy, and full (not still feel great!).
Pain Points	Too many things to do! Don't want to work more—feel that they have been working so much so looking for fun	None, other than getting up early	SO MANY OPTIONS! But don't want heavy calories. And Jess is a vegan so must find good options for her.	None! (except maybe doing some work later....)
User Insights & Emotions	Frustrated but excited	Tired, but happy! Lots of good workout endorphins.	Overwhelmed and hungry	Happy to catch up after a busy week.
Areas for Improvement	Need some inspiration about where to go!	Connections to healthy food as to not ruin their good progress. What about a great protein bowl!	Direct to Saturday Brunch at Truly Good.	2 Instagram posts + 2 Instagram stories

Kate and Carol think that influencer marketing may be a good addition to their marketing mix. To date, they have created some content, using a small boutique social media firm in the area. Truly Good has a fun and engaging blog and an Instagram account with 4,500 followers. Most of the Instagram content includes photos of the regulars (and sometimes a celebrity or two). They do have a Facebook account that includes the menu and specials. In terms of digital advertising, they have placed a few ads on Facebook and Instagram around specific occasions such as Mother's Day. To engage with potential influencers, they have decided to create a campaign brief (Table 5.4).

Table 5.4 Campaign brief

Campaign name	#TrulyGoodSaturday brunch
Brand overview	Truly Good—a healthy restaurant in Uptown Dallas
Specific product/service	Saturday brunch during the summer months
Influencer description	Dallas area influencers—foodies, fitness instructors, young women (20–30), friendly and approachable, known for having a large group of friends and who like to be out and about on the town
Deliverables for creator	2 Instagram posts + 2 Instagram stories
Content direction	Fun, approachable, healthy, authentic. Clean creative. Preferably colors to match Truly Good's logo and palette
Elements	Include time and dates for brunch; favorite dishes (e.g., avocado toast); include friends and can include dog (since the restaurant is pet friendly)
Links and taglines	This would include all social media links and hashtags
Disclosure	Must include #ad, #sponsored before the link and must include SHOW MORE; must be the first hashtag in the list
Other notes	

When considering social media platform, Instagram was chosen as the primary platform because of the visual elements and because it is very popular with Truly Good's audience. There are several ways to choose influencers. For Truly Good, they knew a few people with between 10,000 and 15,000 followers who had an engaged following and who lived in the area and frequented Truly Good. They also found a Pilates and cycle instructor who built an engaged audience who followed her for her glute workouts online (as well as her high energy in person classes at two area fitness clubs). Truly Good also hired an influencer with a larger following to increase awareness. KPIs included engagement rate, shares, new followers, and ultimately bookings and sales. Obviously, this is a small example, but the principles are essentially the same (Figure 5.4).

Figure 5.4 Campaign elements

The next chapter highlights some of the important issues to consider when implementing the influencer marketing campaign. And it will wrap up with a quick look at the future of influencer marketing (at least as we know it right now).

CHAPTER 6

Implementing Influencer Marketing Campaigns

Fyre Festival Explodes

Of course, any time there is a collaboration between brands and influencers, there is the hope that all turns out positively. However, that is not always the case. Probably, one of the most famous influencer successes *and* misfires is the Fyre Festival. It all depends on how you look at it. Let's start with the basics. The Fyre Festival was billed as a luxury music festival on an island in the Bahamas in 2017. It launched with 10 supermodels to set the tone of luxury who then posted on Instagram. The organizers assembled the most famous (and most expensive) SMIs to attend—about 400 macro- and celebrity influencers who uploaded a simple orange visual on their Instagram with the #fyrefest. This coordinated effort helped the event sell out where tickets started at $1,500 and up. There was a ton of hype. It looked like it would be a massive success.[1]

And it was a disaster! The festival was underfunded and poorly planned. There really was no event—and what was there was a complete bait and switch. Not enough food, lodging, or transportation and the music lineup was practically nonexistent. People were angry. Vendors were left with massive unpaid bills both in the United States and in the Bahamas. The Fyre Festival organizers have since been sued, and the whole debacle has been the subject of a variety of investigations and lawsuits. And the vast majority of the more than 400 influencers had little to no knowledge of the venture and the marketing team. They also did not follow the FTC rules on disclosure. As such, followers lost faith in the ability of influencers to be honest and transparent and really put the whole future of influencer marketing in doubt.

Knowing this, it is vital that while the concepts and ideas behind a campaign are important, the actual implementation and execution of the campaign cannot be ignored. This includes some not so exciting topics like contracts and disclosures and ensuring brand safety (as much as possible) on both sides. But this is the line between failure and success.

Dealing With Social Media Influencers: Creative Control

Once a brand determines the right influencers, it is time for all parties to agree on the details and specific requirements of the campaign. Having an influencer marketing agreement minimizes the chance that something will go wrong. What could go wrong? The influencer could not follow through on the expectations. The brand could not be put in the best light. The deadlines are not met. The influencer (or the brand) could do something to create a PR nightmare. People are not paid. All of this has happened. Getting something formal is the next step. A signed agreement provides both parties with legal protections and transparent expectations.

Start with general campaign expectations. This is where the campaign brief is particularly useful. Remember, it provides all the details about the campaign message, deliverables, and deadlines. However, there is one important concept that is hard for brands who have spent millions of dollars and several years designing their brand image to understand. Creative control. It is a major challenge for brands to "let go" but also something that is vital for authenticity. It's a "Goldilocks" effect—too much control and the content will not be authentic or even very good and too little control and the influencer may not have enough brand knowledge to good an effective job. So, it needs to be "just right" and that will largely depend on the experience of the influencer, the comfort level of the brand, and the length of the relationship. Guard rails on content and the influencer are not a bad thing, if they don't stifle the deliverable and thus the campaign outcome.

"In terms of content creation, most brands give you a lot of creative freedom. They trust you know your followers the best. They do want high quality photos and if they are looking for content to also feature on their social media, then the brand will usually send over some examples for inspiration on look and feel," said West Gissinger, fitness influencer. "For example, when working for Steve Madden, they outlined the exact intended use for the photos and I was able to go from there."

Legal Considerations: Contracts and Compensation

As brands move from transactional influencer campaigns to more long-term relationships, contracts are starting to look like traditional talent for TV or other advertising. The language is more comprehensive and detailed (sometimes including the length of the post, the period of paid amplification, and the specific type of content like an Instagram post or a TikTok video), as well as the exclusivity rights, confidentiality agreements, and payment terms. Influencers are being referred to as brand spokespeople or brand ambassadors and brands are likely to request participation outside of social media, such as in person appearances. Some contracts are also including morality clauses to guard their brand safety. Importantly, contracts have longer time periods, showing that brands are increasingly engaging influencers on a more relational level.[2] This also leads to a professionalization of the industry—away from direct messaging and e-mails

Clauses to Protect the Brand

Amanda Russell[3] included some great clauses that are appearing in contracts. They include the following:

- Morals clause: This is designed to prohibit certain behavior by the influencer in their private life. This can include drug use and sexual acts. Historically, they were used to uphold public image.
- Disparagement clause: This is designed to restrict what an influencer can say or cannot say about the brand during the campaign and after their contract has ended. For the brand, this allows it to sever the relationship, refuse payment, and seek compensation through legal means if the influencer spreads damaging information.
- Safety clause: this is designed to keep the influencer physically safe and is important for some product categories. Influencers need to abide by the stated safety guidelines especially in public.

between brand managers and SMIs—to more of a structured legal agreement. This should not come as a surprise given the amount of money that brands spend on influencer marketing. Contracts are also including the investigation of fake followers to ensure that the influencer's audience is legitimate and to reduce advertising fraud.

Once the contract terms are developed, it is time to consider compensation. This is where being specific and detailed is required. There are a variety of ways of being compensated—from free products and services to money. Most influencers are getting paid money for posts. Prices can vary based on several criteria such as the number of followers, the engagement rate, and even the type of brand. Other issues to consider is timing. Is this a one-time payment or ongoing payment? If ongoing, for how long? Does the influencer get some money upfront and the rest at the end? Or are there interim payments? How will the campaign be tracked? Promotion codes help direct the influencers work to sales. Other types of links were outlined in Chapter 5 but are important to consider for payment contracts.

In addition to payment, the agreement should also include the degree of exclusivity—whether the influencer works with other brands. What does that look like? Can the influencer work with similar brands? Think about it as a noncompete agreement. Last, make it clear who owns the content. Is the copyright owned by the brand or the influencer? What can the brand do with the content? Hammer out those details early so there are no surprises.

As relationships grow between a brand and influencer, many will become brand ambassadors. This has been discussed a few places in this book, but essentially when an influencer becomes a brand ambassador, the relationship is a bit more exclusive. Some of this can (and does) include social media, but it is not exclusively online. A great example is how Lululemon uses brand ambassadors. These are typically local fitness instructors in specific cities with retail locations who have an in person following as well as a strong social media presence. Lululemon identifies instructors who embody their values and provides them with high-quality merchandise. They include their photos in the stores. In return, the brand ambassadors post and tag when they wear Lululemon apparel and sometimes promote and attend events in store and elsewhere. This is a great way for Lululemon to tap into each instructor's fitness community in an authentic way.[4]

The Role of Intermediaries

In the introduction of the book, I outlined the various players in the ecosystem. When it comes to implementation of campaigns, there are a few that play an outsized role. Influencer marketing agencies and influencer marketplaces are obvious players. Consider the structure of supply and demand. Supply is represented by influencers. Influencers can use agents (like Estate Five for macro-influencers or other agents) to assist matching them with brands and essentially running their business. Influencer marketplaces allow brands and influencers to connect, and some facilitate important tasks like communication, contracting, payment, and measurement. On the demand side are brands. Influencer marketing agencies are there to provide a seamless full-service experience for brands. If the brand is large, there is likely a role for the agency of record (AOR) which are large advertising or digital marketing agencies who work on broader campaigns other than influencer marketing. Brands also often have in-house capabilities for influencer marketing. Depending on the brand and their desire for control (and their budget), they may have influencer teams in house that do everything. Or they may do part of it. The point is that there is no one path to this. Implementing campaigns take a lot of time, energy, and resources. Technology platforms provide value for all sides—tools for creators and influencers to create their content, make money and run their businesses, tools for brands to search for and select collaborators, and tools for social media platforms to provide value to both sides.

Types of Influencer Marketing and Content Marketing Jobs

As a wide open ecosphere, there are a variety of opportunities for those who want to work in influencer marketing. Here is just a few of the options:[5]

(Continued)

Title	Description
Influencer side	
Influencer	Content creators on social media; build and engage with audiences
Influencer marketing manager	Behind the scenes who serves as a contact person for the influencer; manages the campaigns with brands
Influencer marketing strategist	Develops strategy and execute the campaign
Influencer agent	Usually limited to influencers with larger audience, this person helps find deals and negotiates contracts
Brand or agency side	
Content creator	Create content of all types: blogs, e-mail newsletters, social media copy, videos, eBooks, graphic design, podcasts—anything visual or audio
Content strategist	Create content but also conducts strategy on content delivery and promotion; brand guidelines and editorial strategy; measurement
Content marketing manager	Managing the company's content marketing operations including tying content strategy to other digital efforts like SEO and paid media
Digital marketing manager	Managing the company's digital marketing operations; often includes a variety of digital and traditional marketing initiatives
Creative director	Head of the creative team
Marketing data analyst	Designs, collects, and analyzes market research; often acts as an analytics translator
Coordinators and assistants	Typically, entry level or even intern level; assists with getting the work done

Legal Considerations: Disclosures

Influencer marketing can be particularly tough to regulate. Research shows that for native advertising and influencer marketing alike, consumers fail to recognize content as advertising, leading them to respond more favorably to it.[6] That is great for brands but probably not great for consumer welfare. As such, there have been calls for greater regulation and transparency among all types of advertising and sponsored content, from native advertising to influencer marketing. Researchers acknowledge that influencer marketing is a specific case. The relationship of the influencers with the audience—that engagement that creates a more personal connection—could make consumers more likely to disregard sponsored content. Additionally, given the nature of influencer content, influencer may post a photo of a product with little additional information and no disclosure. Where does this fall? There has been no research showing the different effects of disclosure depending on the type of influencer (e.g., celebrity vs. influencer). There seems to be a pressing need for research to understand the public policy implications of influencer marketing.[7] But others argue that consumers don't always appreciate the disclosure. In a 2017 study, survey respondents viewed a brand more negatively when the relationship was disclosed. But by 2018, there was really no difference. There was no difference in trust and no difference in intentions to buy. Given that influencer marketing is moving quickly, even data from 2018 may prove to be dated. So ideally, as authenticity importance increases, disclosures may also become vital.[8] Newer research shows that disclosures can enhance rather than detract from consumer-based outcomes.[9]

In 2019, the FTC devised and disseminated regulation and disclosure policies for influencer marketing. The premise to influencers: if you endorse a product through social media (meaning you are paid or provided something of value), then you have a relationship with the brand, called a material connection. A material connection to a brand includes a personal, family, or employment relationship or financial relationship such as the brand paying or giving you free or discounted products or services.[10] The FTC has constructed strict rules about endorsement and disclosure. This is important since brands don't always want influencers to disclose their financial arrangements (given the efficacy of influencer marketing). One study showed that 28 percent of influencers were requested by their sponsoring brands not to disclose the relationship.[11] However, most reputable brands understand the importance (and several high-profile enforcement cases have added to the effect).

Sponsored content and sponsored social aren't exactly like other forms of advertising (even native advertising). Most people have a tough time identifying sponsored social by an influencer because it matches the tone and language of the influencer's content. Another key difference is that content is not developed by the brand but rather by the influencer. Influencers typically have control of the look and feel to maximize

What to Disclose and How[13]

When to disclose	When there is a relationship (e.g., you have been paid or received free products/services) Remember tags, likes, pins, etc. are also endorsements
How to disclose	Place it where it is hard to miss Content = message Photo = superimpose the disclosure Video = superimpose the disclosure Live stream = repeat it often Use simple and clear language (ad, sponsored) or #ad #sponsored. Don't use vague or confusing terms
What else to know	You can't talk about the experience unless you have tried it Even if you are paid, if the product is terrible you can't say it was great You can't make up claims about a product that would require proof that a brand does not have

authenticity for their audiences. There are six types of sponsored content, all of which require disclosure. Product reviews are when a brand sends a product to an influencer to review it. "Like" a brand of "Follow" a brand on social media is more of an implicit endorsement, but an endorsement, nevertheless. Marketers have hired influencers to do both for years. Product placement in sponsored content is probably one of the most popular types right now. A post features a product or service (or even simply mentioned). Unboxing videos (and haul videos) are where influencers are sent products and then video themselves unboxing it. Maybe strange, but popular. Social media takeovers have been around for a while, but essentially an influencer is given free reign over a brand's Snapchat, for example. Creative campaigns can take multiple forms and often do include multiple posts and stories. If money or free products and services exchange hands, then the influencer must disclose it.[12]

One consideration—regulations are different in different countries. So, if the campaign is international, the other country's regulations must also be included. Chances are those campaigns are for bigger brands who are using agencies who have more resources to ensure that accountability level.

Ethical Considerations: Fake Followers and Influencer Fraud

One of the biggest concerns that brands have about influencers is whether the number of followers and the engagement rates are real and whether the influencer is real. It is easy and cheap to purchase followers and early on, this was a huge problem. These are generated by bots and can look quite real. In 2017, influencer agency Mediakix created two completely fictitious Instagram accounts—one for a lifestyle and fashion model and the other for a travel photographer. They posted daily and then started purchasing fake followers. With minimal investment, one account grew to more than 30,000 followers. They also purchased engagement in the form of comments and likes. After they got it started, they joined a few influencer marketplaces and applied for a few opportunities and were accepted. The whole point of the experiment was to show how easy creating fake influencers and faking followers can be. Each of these opportunities came with compensation and most of the brands did not suspect a thing.

How to spot a fake? Check out their followers. Do they appear to have any interest or connection to the influencer? Do they have names and avatars that sound like the influencer's name? Or are there long lists of names and numbers that just look strange? Check on those followers and see if any have no posts or posts that look the same. Fake influencers will use automation and borrowed content to populate their feed and links to give the appearance of activity. Also look for conversations (not only comments) among followers to see if they are real. Watch out for short comments that are useless and repeated comments from the same person. The big lesson here? If you are influencer, don't try to fake it. And if you are a brand, do your homework.

Unintended Consequences

Given that influencer marketing is increasingly important but still relatively new, there are inevitably negative issues to consider. As brands, platforms, creators, influencers, and even governing bodies define the ecosystem, mistakes are bound to happen. Major issues include the issue of brand safety (for both brands and influencers) and cases of deceit, and vulnerable audiences can cause problems and should be considered when implementing campaigns.

Brand safety is the ability for a brand to avoid content that is inappropriate for advertising and unfit for publisher monetization regardless of the advertisement or brand.[14] For brands, brand safety is crucial. Brands take crisis communication and PR scandals quite seriously, and they don't want to be caught up in controversy, especially from an influencer. This is increasingly important as scandals around brands can lead to the loss of millions of dollars. As such, vetting influencers has become much more rigorous than in the past. "There is a lot of hesitation and caution and more vetting criteria being added to contracts because brands are terrified of having a negative halo effect from an influencer mistake," said Addi McCauley at IZEA.[15] She adds that vetting influencers is probably one of the biggest aspects of launching a campaign, especially for large brands and for conservative brands. "They are asking us to go back through several years' worth of posts—I mean, that is not the norm, but some brands are looking for certain topics and we are doing comprehensive searches on influencers. The normal litmus test for most brands is 30 and 60 days."[16]

JetBlue Airlines is an example of a brand who experienced negative backlash due to an influencer campaign. However, in this case, it wasn't the influencers' fault. The campaign was a sweepstakes that awarded influencers the chance to win free travel for one year. JetBlue asked the influencers to archive their posts and upload the JetBlue image from the content website along with a branded hashtag. The intention was for users to see the JetBlue material across several accounts, but the sponsored posts lacked clarity about what the contest involved causing a lot of negative comments and confusion. Additionally, JetBlue did not announce the winners, leading to more anger. The campaign lacked authenticity and influencers were not provided with enough detail to execute on it effectively.[17]

Given the events of the last few years, social issues—especially social justice—have garnered increased attention. "There are massive conversations for better or worse happening around cultural topics and political topics and brands are synthesizing that and want their brand content to be there," said Addi McCauley at IZEA. "Some of these conversations are very positive but also some are very negative and filled with hate. How do we synthesize that from a brand safety perspective? It comes to vetting who works with you and that these are real people because you may have a brand that worked with an influencer and then four months later, they go and say something inappropriate and then there are people trying to cancel that brand because they worked with them. Sometimes it is hard to know if it was intentional or an accidental misstep by the influencer." McCauley cited an example of a well-known influencer in her field with more than a million followers on Instagram who was attacked because of a donation to a political candidate. She added that would have been a nightmare for any brand working with her at the time.[18]

Given the issues around the pandemic and social justice, both brands and influencers feel the need to say something. Some brands were voicing support of issues around the pandemic such as testing and vaccines and voicing support for social justice and issues around diversity. Despite these topics being controversial in some circles, some brands seem to feel that it is needed for their relevancy. Influencers used their voices to raise awareness around nonprofits and different organizations around the same topics. In many cases, their audiences were expecting them to say something, and if they did not say something, it would cause more trouble than if they did. Interestingly, prior to 2020, if influencers were discussing sensitive topics around social justice, they ran the real risk that brands would stay away. That changed in 2020.

Brand safety is also important to the influencer. They don't want to be associated with a brand that has garnered negative attention since this can backfire on their audience's perceptions of their authenticity. Influencers have worked hard to build up their following and engagement, especially around specific topics that they talk about and that brands talk about. The topics that resonate most with followers is what influencers are willing to partner with brands about. Most influencers are not going to partner with a brand just for the money unless it fits with their values and topic areas. "Micro influencers and nano influencers are not taking a deal if it wasn't something that truly does authentically resonates with them," said Addi McCauley. "These influencers are not going to alienate their entire audiences for something that they would normally not talk about."

However, influencers also make mistakes and don't follow through on their obligations. Kim Kardashian failed to disclose potential side effects of a morning sickness medicine, violating Food and Drug Administration (FDA) standards. She had to issue correction and amend the post. Bethany Mota failed to uphold her contract with Studio71. She agreed to promote a skincare brand on YouTube for $325,000 and she failed to do it and Studio71 filed a lawsuit. Others have been burned by their past comments. PewDiePie has had a few influencer fails including racially insensitive comments. Same with beauty YouTuber Laura Lee who apologized for racists Tweets going back to 2012. Some are just silly. Influencer Scott Disick (of Kardashian fame) cut and pasted his campaign instructions directly to his Instagram showing a shocking lack of detail. Actions like this actually hurts both the influencer and the brand involved (in this case Bootea, a brand that sells fitness and detox products). Sadly, the same thing occurred with Naomi Campbell and Adidas. And then, there are the major scandals. Olivia Jade Giannulli lost most of her endorsements after the Varsity Blues college admission scandal. While the target of the investigation was her parents, her comments about only going to college for the parties and the football games did not help her reputation.[19] The Fyre Festival covered at the beginning of the chapter outlines outright deceit, in this case from the "brand" but also showed a lack of due diligence from influencers.

Another issue to consider is who is online. While this is far greater than influencer marketing, most social media platforms require users to be 13, but we know that many of the users on Instagram, Snapchat, and TikTok are much younger. Are there unintended consequences to consider? Younger users can certainly follow influencers who may not share content in a PG manner. Younger users can be exposed to language and content they are not ready for. There can also be issues such as social comparison and fear of missing out (FOMO) that can also affect how users are reacting to social media. As such, influencers should at least consider who is in their audience and why.

Future of Influencer Marketing

So, what is next? What is the future of influencer marketing? "Our CMO who is really, really smart and who has been in this space for a long time said 'find me somebody who says they're an expert in influencer marketing and I'll show you a liar'," said Lynsey Eaton, cofounder and CEO of Estate Five. "Things are constantly changing and what we need to do is be nimble and ready and willing to open up doors and run through doors and stick our heads in and be find out what's going on and try anything."[20] Just consider how much activity has happened in the past few years! Hundreds of millions of dollars in investment, hundreds of start-up companies in the space, and millions of new influencers and brands who are finally realizing the value of authentic communication. It will be interesting to see what happens. Generally, however, there are few areas to watch.[21]

Platforms

Platforms come and go. There are already new ones rising. Clubhouse, the audio-only social media platform, is a great example and brands are starting to look at the possibilities there. Andrea Arias mentioned that Cetaphil is looking at Clubhouse for potential. Addi McCauley mentioned that some of the clients at IZEA are exploring it, and Lynsey Eaton said that it is something they are reviewing as well. Instagram launched Reels as a competitor to TikTok. The growth of TikTok in such a short amount of time is a good indicator of how fast things will move. Other platforms will focus on diverse audiences. Dubsmash is a great example of a platform that has been around since 2014 where 70 percent of the content is created by females and more than 25 percent of Black teens use it. Some platforms will see a resurgence. "People are starting to come back on Pinterest," said Eaton. "Randomly we have been getting these contracts that are Pinterest only campaigns. Pinterest itself has been working with influencers to try and create more awareness about the brand and are having influencers create Pinterest exclusive content."[22]

Technology

Data and planning will rule the day. This will include performance-based contracts and deals in order to maximize return on investment. Artificial intelligence (AI) and machine learning will enable brands and influencers to accomplish more in less time. This will include a greater ability to track and measure influence and ultimate success from the brand's perspective. eCommerce solutions like shoppable videos and posts will become more important as brands are able to draw direct lines from influencer to sales while also creating a seamless experience for customers. Think about it. An entire consumer journey can occur on one platform.

Technology such as neuromarketing (uses functional magnetic resonance imaging (MRI) to study the brand's reactions to marketing stimuli) could help marketers select an influencer who resonates.[23] Wearable devices like the Apple watch can provide a different kind of influence on buyer behavior (that in a day redefines influencer marketing away from social media).[24] And there are more AR (augmented reality) filters that allow for more effects on Instagram.

Specialization

Influencers will start to carve out niches and develop specific expertise and trust in an area making them even more sought after by brands. There will be a greater emphasis on the "creator" part of it rather than only the "influencer" part of their roles. Content houses have been around since YouTube developed them to create an environment for creators and influencers to make video content. Jake Paul's Team 10 and Clout House are two earlier examples. Recently, TikTok content houses have become popular. Hype House and Sway House (both LA based) launched the careers of several major TikTok influencers.[25] The Crib around the corner is the only Black TikTok house and is home to five Black creators which is sponsored by AT&T TV. This will inevitably lead to more creator collaborations.

Diversity

Brands are reaching out to more diverse influencers. IZEA's earlier information on the state of the creator economy (Chapter 2) showed that Black and Latinx influencers are in high demand. "More and more there is a definitely brands have asked for more diverse influencers. I think that brands understand that in their marketing in general, they need to stop showing only skinny white blonde women," said Addi McCauley of IZEA. "We have run campaigns that are very specifically all Hispanic influencers or all influencers of color across different ethnicities." McCauley added that more multicultural agencies are popping up to reach specific types of communities of color.[26] As brands embrace diversity and inclusion, they will have to determine who to partner with and how to meet their goals. But more is needed. Social media platforms (like TikTok and Instagram) have faced criticism about their lack of diverse audiences and influencers leaving an opportunity for new platforms and new influencers. Look for brands to try to change that (e.g., AT&T TV).

New Influencers

One thing seems to be for sure. Brands will be looking to influencers with smaller audiences but greater engagement. Micro- and nano-influencers will continue to grow, meaning that more and more "everyday people" can become influencers in their own space. This also allows marketing budgets to stretch further and increase their return on investment. "Smaller influencers are great because they are going to work hard for you (the brand) because they are honored to have a chance to show what they are worth and their content creation will have great photos and video assets of the product in all kinds of settings from all kinds of people from all walks of life and if you are really a brand focused on quality-based marketing and accessing the widest audience possible, that makes a lot of sense for your business," said Ryan Schram, COO IZEA. "It's not only economically feasible, it's also very rational in terms of where we are as a society."[27]

Brands will start pushing toward using other types of influencers such as the AI-generated "people" discussed earlier in the book. Digital avatars like Miquela Sousa (Lil Miquela) is a good example. This further blurs the lines of reality and artificiality in the online personas of influencers and celebrities. Additional uses of AI and VR (virtual reality) will continue to allow to do more than consumer content. They will be able to experience it. Technologies like Live Streaming will become more popular allowing influencers to get even closer to their audiences.[28]

College Athletes as the New
Social Media Influencers

Things are changing in college sports. As the NCAA continues to grapple with rules allowing athletes to earn outside compensation for NIL (name, image, likeness), several states have moved forward with allowing athletes to be paid by third parties for sponsorships, online endorsements, and personal appearances. A recent Supreme Court decision made the NCAA more vulnerable to antitrust cases and as such, the NCAA has opted for a more hands off approach to players seeking outside compensation. There is no doubt that college athletes will take to social media to become influencers. Many student athletes already have thousands of followers and not just from their own school. Agencies and organizations will help student athletes to capitalize on influencer marketing. Aside from some state laws, the NCAA policies are set up to be able to match an athlete to their interests. Companies and technology platforms have emerged to help athletes navigate this new world. Dreamfield is one example that allows businesses to browse the platform to hire for five categories of events including meet and greets, autograph sessions, and paid speeches. The rates are set by the athletes and are not negotiable. The organization will also help with payment, contracts, and tax implications.[29]

Other companies are helping athletes develop their image. For example, the University of Nebraska and athlete marketing program Opendorse developed a program called Ready Now to assist athletes with individual branding to market themselves as social media influencers. This includes all athletes—not just the visible ones like football and basketball. Those who spoke to the blog FiveThirtyEight "were adamant that once NIL rights are permitted by the NCAA, influencer marketing via social media will be the primary money-making vehicle of the modern day student athlete, one that will dominate at least an initial wave of transactions."[30]

Influencer marketing firm Captiv8 put out one of the first influencer marketing playbooks for creators, specifically aimed at athletes that included a primer on influencer marketing and ways to make money—from sponsored posts, affiliate marketing, competitions and giveaways, long-term ambassadors, and even product collaboration. Researchers believe that the largest sum of money will go to football and basketball players given their name recognition. That said, many experts believe that the eased restrictions will benefit female athletes who have had fewer money-making opportunities in professional sports relative to men. But many do have a large and loyal following. So expect major disruption and innovation in this space in the near future.

"We're not getting paid salaries," said McKenzie Milton, Florida State's quarterback. "It's profiting off your name, image and likeness, which is what any other college student can do while being a social media influencer, while going out to work in their communities."[31]

Relationships

Following best practices to date and taking into consideration authenticity and brand safety, brand will likely develop relationships with influencers, rather than single transactional campaigns. This gets into the earlier endorser models (e.g., Michael Jordan and Nike) where the endorser became synonymous with the brand, at least in basketball circles. Obviously, Nike did this well. Can other brands build effective relationships with influencers that maximize their return on investment while also allowing the influencer to remain true to his or her audience?

This can ultimately lead to new ways of collaborating. The typical influencer who is only focused on social media is giving way to a broader perspective on the concept of a creator. As such, influencers could be partners in product development and extension, new businesses, and start-ups, featured in major traditional media, subject matter experts, and strategists.[32]

Multiple Revenue Streams

Social media platforms are revisiting some of their regulations and providing more ways for creators to make money. Instagram announced a new affiliate program that allows creators to earn money from product promotions. This is in addition to its Stars creator donations process. Facebook has announced that it will allow creators to earn ad revenue on short videos. Additionally, it will allow creators to use its tools like paid subscriptions and paid online events through 2023, and then when it does charge, it will be lower than some of the competition (namely Apple who charges 30 percent). Snapchat has been paying $1 million per day to creators who make viral short videos on its feature called Snapchat Spotlight. Twitter recently announced it would launch "Super Follows," which would let users charge followers for exclusive content. YouTube shares ad revenue with video makers. Social media platforms are realizing that they need creators who are essentially providing the value of the network.

Backlash

Authenticity will remain one of the most powerful considerations for both brands and influencers. As such, partnerships and collaborations as well as creative control of the messaging will become more and more important. This idea of authenticity will likely clash some with disclosure requirements. That means campaign structure will go beyond sponsored posts, and it will be difficult for audience members to determine if their favorite influencer loves the brand for real or are they just being paid to create a different type of content.

A different kind of backlash is around cancel culture. How will brands and influencers handle the growing political divide and the loud voices of people who want to cancel things they don't agree with it. Social activism will become more important. Brands will have to decide their point of view on many topics—many related to social justice—and influencers will also have to decide their own point of view. Pressure will come to both sides on taking stands on political and social issues, which could leave some brands and influencers with unhappy audiences.

Future Research Areas

From an academic perspective, there is still so much to be learned about influencer marketing. For example, there is still more development needed on some tried and true concepts like trust, expertise, liking, attractiveness, and similarity. Additionally, there is a huge need to better understand the role of authenticity in influencer marketing. This is something that differs from celebrities and macro-endorsers. More research needs to be done on brand safety and subsequent backlash when things go awry. Brand safety should be examined for both parties. Typically, when we think of brand safety, the company comes to mind. But each influencer is a brand, and they also have concerns about backlash due to collaborations and partnerships. More work needs to be done on disclosures and their effectiveness. Researchers can also examine the differential effects on various audiences. Are there some audiences who are more susceptible to influencers? Are there negative implications like social comparisons to an unrealistic ideal? Are there other theories that better explain influencer marketing than the ones we have adapted from celebrity endorsement? Perhaps, there are new theories to be developed that can explain the effectiveness of influencer marketing.

"It is laughable to put some timestamp on what is going to happen because if you had told me that those same contemporaries would be making millions of dollars based on the same content that they would be posting and it would have lasted this long, it sounds insane. A lot of this is tech driven and not predictable," said Eaton. "But I am hopeful. I am hopeful that there will be more accountability. I am hopeful that people will have more respect for the creators themselves and the actual work they are doing, because it is hard. And I am hopeful that there will still be growth and more understanding and more collaboration between the brands and the creators."

Notes

Introduction

1. Collings 2021 and Collings (April 30, 2020).
2. Russell (2020).
3. Schaffer (2020).
4. Schaffer (2020).
5. Kelman (1958).
6. Cialdini (2021).
7. Russell (2020).
8. Russell (2020).
9. Russell (2020).
10. Berger (October 2014).
11. Berger (October 2014).
12. Schaffer (2020).
13. Berstein (May 24, 2019); IZEA (n.d.)and Kim (January 14, 2020).
14. Interview with Ryan Schram, COO and President IZEA. April 24, 2021.
15. Interview with Ryan Schram, COO and President IZEA .April 24, 2021.
16. Kim (2020).
17. Interview with Addi McCauley, IZEA. February 05, 2021.
18. Russell (2020).
19. N.A. (2021).
20. Appel, Grewal, Rhonda, and Stephen (2002).
21. Schaffer (2020).
22. N.A (2021).
23. N.A (2021).

Chapter 1

1. How the NFL Tackles Gen Z Through Social Media Platforms with Tim Ellis, Executive Vice President and Chief Marketing Officer NFL; Iman Trombetta, Senior VP, Social and Influencer Marketing NFL and Aubrey Peacock, Manager Social Content Strategy, NFL. Social Media Week LA from AdWeek. June 29, 2021.
2. Statista (2021).
3. Voorveld and Hilde (2019).

4. N.A. (September 23, 2020).

5. Appel, Grewal, Hadi and Stephen (2002).

6. Henderson (2020).

7. Iqbal (2021).

8. Iqbal (2020).

9. Quesenberry (2020).

10. Wurmser (2019).

11. Schaffer (2020).

12. Schaffer (2020).

13. Rimmer (n.d.).

14. Alhabash, Mundel and Hussain (2017).

15. N.A. (2021).

16. N.A. (2021).

17. N.A. (2020).

18. Quesenberry (2020).

19. N.A. (2021).

20. N.A. (2021).

21. N.A. (2021).

22. Campbell and Grimm (2019).

23. Wojdynski and Evans (2016).

24. N.A. (2021).

25. N.A. (2021).

26. N.A. (2021).

27. N.A. (2021).

28. Campbell and Grimm (2019).

29. Freeman, Spencer, and Bird (2012).

30. Schaffer (2020).

31. N.A. (2021).

32. N.A. (2021).

33. Campbell and Farrell (2020).

34. N.A. (2021).

35. Vaughan (2016).

36. N.A. (2021).

37. Taylor (2021).

38. N.A. (2020).

39. Taylor (2021).

40. Taylor (2021).

41. N.A. (2021).

42. Taylor (2021).

43. Young (2020).

Chapter 2

1. Interview, West Gissinger, July 20, 2021.
2. Van Kaspar (2020) and Murphy (2020).
3. Bergendorff (2021).
4. Yuanling and Constine (n.d.).
5. N.A. (May 15, 2021).
6. Princewall (2021).
7. Bergendorff (2021).
8. Bergendorff (2021).
9. Bergendorff (2021).
10. Princewall (2021).
11. N.A. (September 23, 2020).
12. Schram (2020).
13. Bergendorff (2021).
14. Jin (2020).
15. Yang (2020).
16. Jin (2020).
17. Yang (2020).
18. Jin (2020).
19. N.A. (September 23, 2021).
20. N.A. (May 13, 2021).
21. N.A. (May 13, 2021).
22. N.A. (2018).
23. N.A. (2021).
24. N.A. (2021).
25. N.A. (2021).
26. N.A. (2021).
27. N.A. (2021).
28. Thimothy (2021).
29. Yang (2020).
30. Bergendorff (2021) and Princewall (2021).
31. Bergendorff (2021).
32. Princewall (2021).
33. N.A. (June 12, 2019).
34. N.A. (August 19, 2019).
35. Maltby (2020).
36. N.A. (September 23, 2021).
37. N.A. (2020).
38. Hutcheson (2019).

Chapter 3

1. (Re)volution of Rockstar Energy Drink, Gabe Alonso, Head of Digital Platforms and Community, PepsiCo, Social Media Week LA, Adweek, June 29, 2021.
2. Katz and Lazersfeld (1955).
3. Valsesia, Proserpio, and Nunes (2020).
4. Valsesia, Proserpio, and Nunes (2020).
5. Lin, Bruning and Bruning (2018).
6. Katz and Lazersfeld (1955).
7. Erdogan (1999).
8. Knoll and Matthes (2017).
9. Amos, Holmes, and Strutton (2008); Bergkvist and Qiang Zhou (2016); Carrillat and Illicit (2019); Knoll and Matthes (2017) and Schimmelpfennig and Hunt (2020).
10. Boorstin (1961).
11. Driessens (2013).
12. Carrillat and Illicit (2019).
13. McCracken (1989).
14. Bergkvist and Qiang Zhou (2016).
15. Carrillat and Illicit (2019).
16. Khamis, Ang, and Welling (2016) and De Veirman, Cauberghe, and Hudders (2017).
17. De Veirman, Cauberghe, and Hudders (2017).
18. Evans, Phua, Lim, and Jun (2017).
19. Campbell and Farrell (2020).
20. N.A. (2021).
21. Delbaere, Michael, and Phillips (2021).
22. Lou and Yuan (2019).
23. Freberg, Graham, McGaughey, and McGaughey (n.d.).
24. Berryman and Kavka (2017) and Khamis, Ang, and Welling (2016).
25. Lou and Yuan (2019).
26. McCracken (1989) and Kay, Mulcahy, and Parkinson (2020).
27. De Veirman, Cauberghe, and Hudders (2017); Evans, Phua, Lim, and Jun (2017); and Kay, Mulcahy and Parkinson (2020).
28. N.A. (2021).
29. N.A. (2021).
30. N.A. (2021).
31. All examples of influencers from Mediakix (www.mediakix.com/blog).
32. N.A. (2021).
33. Shaffer (2020).

34. Interview, West Gissinger, July 20, 2021.
35. Shaffer (2020).
36. www.izea.com
37. Stevenson (2021).
38. N.A. (2021).
39. N.A. (2021).
40. Haenlein, Anadol, Farnsworth, Hugo, Hunichen, and Welte (2020).
41. Shaffer (2020).
42. Valsesia, Proserpio, and Nunes (2020).
43. Feng (2016).
44. De Veirman, Cauberghe, and Hudders (2017).
45. Appel, Grewal, Hadi, and Stephen (2020).
46. Nguyen (2020).
47. Addi McCauley interview Friday April 23, 2021.
48. Thomas and Fowler (2021).
49. Thomas and Fowler (2021).

Chapter 4

1. Normalizing the conversation: How Headspace and Content Creators Have Helped Destigmatize Mental Health to Improve the Health and Happiness of the World. Val Kaplan, Chief Marketing Officer, Headspace; Natalie Silverstein, Senior VP and Head of Innovation, Collectively Inc., and Chrissy Rutherford, Fashion and Social Media Expert. Social Media Week LA, *AdWeek*, June 29, 2021.
2. Choi and Rifon (2007).
3. Ohanian (1990).
4. Hovland, Janis, and Kelley (1953).
5. McGuire (1985).
6. Ohanian (1990).
7. Bergkvist and Qiang Zhou (2016) and Eisend and Langner (2010) and Ohanian (1991).
8. McGinnies and Ward (n.d.).
9. Wang and Scheinbaum (2018).
10. Siemens, Smith, Fisher, and Jensen (2018).
11. Eisend and Langner (2010).
12. Biswas, Biswas, and Das (2006).
13. Lafferty, Goldsmith, and Flynn (2005).
14. Erdogan, Baker, and Tagg (2001); Kahle and Homer (1985) and Kamins (1990).
15. Schimmelpfennig and Hunt (2020).

16. McGuire (1985).
17. Choi and Rifon (2007).
18. Bergkvist and Qiang Zhou (2016); Eisend and Langner (2010) and Ohanian (1991).
19. Djafarova and Rushworth (2017).
20. Schouten, Janssen, and Verspaget (2020).
21. Chung and Cho (2017).
22. Breves, Liebers, Abt, and Kunze (2019).
23. De Veirman, Cauberghe and Hudders (2017).
24. Lou and Yuan (2019) and Yuan and Lou (2020).
25. N.A. (2021).
26. Kapitan and Silvera (2016).
27. Breves, ole Liebers, Abt, and Kunze (2019).
28. Schouten, Janssen and Verspaget (2020).
29. Yuan and Lou (2020).
30. N.A. (2021).
31. Sander (2021).
32. Interview Andrea Arias, Associate Brand manager Cetaphil, June 12, 2021.
33. N.A. (2021).
34. Riot Games (2021).
35. Torres, Augusto, and Matos (2019).
36. Breves, Liebers, Abt, and Kunze (2019).
37. De Veirman, Cauberghe, and Hudders (2017).
38. Schouten, Janssen, and Verspaget (2020).
39. Schimmelpfennig and Hunt (2020).
40. Kahle and Homer (1985) and Kamins (1990).
41. Lynch and Schuler (1994).
42. Schimmelpfennig and Hunt (2020).
43. Kamins (1990) and Till and Busler (1998).
44. Kamins (1990); Lynch and Schuler (1994) and Till and Busler (1998).
45. Choi and Rifon (2012) and Erdogan, Zaffer, Baker, and Tagg (2001).
46. Breves, Liebers, Abt, and Kunze (2019).
47. Breves, Liebers, Abt, and Kunze (2019).
48. Schouten, Janssen and Verspaget (2020).
49. McCracken (1989).
50. Bergkvist and Zhou (2016).
51. Schimmelpfennig and Hunt (2020).
52. Batra and Homer (2014); Campbell and Warren (2012) and Miller and Allen (2012).
53. Wong, Fock and Ho (2020).
54. Torres, Augusto and Matos (2019).

55. All stats from "Changing the Game: Influencer Marketing for Generation Z" from *Influencer Marketing Hub*.
56. Horton and Wohl (1956).
57. Yuan and Lou (2020).
58. Bond (2016) and Bond (2018).
59. Yuan and Lou (2020).
60. Addi McCauley interview, IZEA April 25, 2021.
61. Chung and Cho (2017).
62. Ferchaud, Orme and LaGroue (2018).
63. Kim and Song (2016).
64. Kim and Song (2016).
65. Tu (n.d.).
66. Eggins and Slade (1997).
67. Rourke, Anderson, Garrison and Archer (2001).
68. Cohen and Tyler (2016).
69. Audrezet, de Kerviler, and Moulard (2020).

Chapter 5

1. N.A. (2021).
2. Russell (2020).
3. N.A. (2021).
4. Solis (n.d.).
5. Solis (n.d.).
6. Solis (n.d.).
7. Russell (2020).
8. N.A. (2021).
9. Solis (n.d.).
10. Haenlein and Anadol (2020).
11. Influencer Marketing Success Playbook.
12. Lynsey Eaton interview, Estate Five, June 10, 2021.
13. Andrea Arias interview, Cetaphil, June 11, 2021.
14. Brittany Knight, Nike, interview June 14, 2021.
15. West Gissinger, Session Pilates, interview July 20, 2021.
16. Russell (2020).
17. Haenlein, Anadol, Farnsworth, Hugo, Hunichen and Welte (2020).
18. Liberating the creative voice: working authentically with influencers, Karyn Spencer, Chief Marketing Officer, Whaler and Nick Bianchi, Director, Digital and Social Media, AT&T in Adweek's Social Media Week LA, June 30, 2021.
19. Harold (2020).

20. N.A. (2021).
21. Haenlein, Anadol, Farnsworth, Hugo, Hunichen, and Welte (2020).
22. Instagram by the Numbers: Stats, Demographics and fun Facts.
23. Barker (n.d.).
24. N.A. (2021).
25. N.A. (2021).
26. N.A. (2021).
27. Monllos (2021).
28. Monllos (2021).
29. N.A. (2021).
30. Pavlovskaya (2021).
31. Haenlein, Anadol, Farnsworth, Hugo, Hunichen and Welte (2020).
32. Shaffer (2020).
33. Russell (2020).
34. Shaffer (2020).
35. Hiebert (2021).
36. Shaffer (2020).
37. Russell (2020).
38. Russell (2020).
39. Influencer Marketing must do's from the best in business (and how you can adopt them), Begley, cofounder and president, Trybe Dynamics and McCorquodale, Executive Vice President Revenue, Trybe Dynamics. Adweek's Social Media Week LA, July 01, 2021; Kathyn (2021).
40. How Google is Evaluating Return on Influencer Marketing. Tobias Rauscher, Global Influencer Marketing Lead, Google, Adweek's Social Media Week LA, June 30, 2021.
41. Truly Good is a fictitious example.

Chapter 6

1. Kaur (2019).
2. Liefreing (2018).
3. Russell (2020).
4. The Ultimate Guide to Influencer Marketing, Meltwater.
5. Geyser (2020) and N.A. (2019).
6. Campbell and Grimm (2019).
7. Kees and Andrews (2019).
8. Audrezet and Charry (2019).
9. Kay, Mulcahy and Parkinson (2020).
10. Disclosure 101 for Social Media Influencers. Federal Trade Commission.
11. Audrezet and Charry (2019).

12. www.izea.com

13. Disclosure 101 for Social Media Influencers. Federal Trade Commission; www.ftc.gov/influencers

14. Internet Advertising Bureau www.iab.com

15. Addi McCauley interview, IZEA, Feb 5, 2021.

16. Addi McCauley interview, IZEA, April 23, 2021.

17. N.A. (2021).

18. Addi McCauley interview, IZEA, April 23, 2021.

19. N.A. (2021).

20. Lynsey Eaton interview, Estate Five, June 10, 2021.

21. N.A. (2021).

22. Lynsey Eaton interview, Estate Five, June 10, 2021.

23. Russell (2020).

24. Russell (2020).

25. The Ultimate TikTok house list, www.kapwing.com/resources/tiktok-houses-list/

26. Addi McCauley interview, IZEA, April 23, 2021.

27. Ryan Schram interview, IZEA May 21, 2021.

28. Russell (2020).

29. Blinder (2021).

30. Planos (2021).

31. Blinder (2021).

32. Russell (2020).

References

Alhabash, S., J. Mundel, and S.A. Hussain. 2017. "Social Media Advertising: Unraveling the Mystery Box." In *Digital Advertising: Theory and Research*, eds. S. Rodgers and E. Thorson, pp. 285–299. New York, NY: Routledge.

Amos, C., G. Holmes and D. Strutton. 2008. "Exploring the Relationship Between Celebrity Endorser Effects and Advertising Effectiveness: A Quantitative Synthesis of Effect Size." *International Journal of Advertising* 27, no. 2, pp. 209–234.

Appel, G., Grewal, L., Rhonda, H, and A.T. Stephen. 2002. "The future of social media in marketing." *Journal of the Academy of Marketing Science* 48, pp. 79–95.

Audrezet, A., and K. Charry. August 29, 2019. "Do Influencers Need to Tell Audiences They're Getting Paid." *Harvard Business Review*. https://hbr.org/2019/08/do-influencers-need-to-tell-audiences-theyre-getting-paid (accessed June 10, 2021).

Audrezet, A., G. de Kerviler, and J.G. Moulard. 2020. "Authenticity Under Threat: When Social Media Influencers Need to Go Beyond Self Presentation." *Journal of Business Research* 117, pp. 557–569.

Barker, S. n.d. "A Comprehensive Guide to Instagram Influencer Marketing." *Convince & Convert*. www.convinceandconvert.com/social-media-strategy/guidelines (accessed June 01, 2021).

Barker, S. March 18, 2021. "5 Influencer Marketing Fails You Can Learned from (updated 2021)." http://shanebarker.com/blog/influencer-marketing-fails

Batra, R., and P. Homer. 2014. "The Situational Impact of Brand Beliefs." *Journal of Consumer Psychology* 14, no. 3, pp. 318–330.

Begley, C., Co-founder and president, Trybe Dynamics and Brit McCorquodale, Executive Vice President Revenue, Trybe Dynamics. Adweek's Social Media Week LA, July 01, 2021; Lundstrom, K. July 06, 2021. "These Beauty Brands are Nailing Influencer Marketing in 2021." *Adweek*. www.adweek.com/brand-marketing/these-beauty-brands-are-nailing-influencer-marketing-in-2021 (accessed July 09, 2021).

Berger, J. October, 2014. "Word of Mouth and Interpersonal Communication." *Journal of Consumer Psychology*, pp. 586–607.

Bergendorff, C.L. March 12, 2021. "From the Attention Economy to the Creator Economy: A Paradigm Shift." *Forbes*. www.forbes.com/sites/claralindhbergendorff/2021/03/12/ (accessed April 09, 2021).

Bergkvist, L. and K.Q. Zhou. 2016. "Celebrity Endorsements: A Literature Review and Research Agenda." *International Journal of Advertising* 35, no. 4, pp. 642–663.

Berryman, R., and M. Kavka. 2017. "I Guess a Lot of People See Me as Big Sister or a Friend: The Role of Intimacy in the Celebrification of Beauty Vloggers." *Journal of Gender Studies* 26, no. 3, pp. 307–320.

Biswas, D., A. Biswas, and N. Das. 2006. "The Differential Effects of Celebrity and Expert Endorsements on Consumer Risk Perceptions: The Role of Consumer Knowledge, Perceived Congruency and Product Technology Orientation." *Journal of Advertising* 35, no. 2, pp. 17–31.

Blinder, A. July 1, 2021. "College Athletes Cash In on Generations of Rules Fade Under Pressure." *The New York Times.* www.nytimes.com/2021/07/01/sports/ncaafootball/ncaa-college-athletes-endorsements.html (accessed July 09, 2021).

Bond, B.J. 2016. "Following Your Friend: Social Media and the Strength of Adolescents' Para-Social Relationships with Media Personae." *Cyberpsychology, Behavior and Social Networking* 19, no. 11, pp. 656–660.

Bond, B.J. 2018. "Para-Social Relationships with Media Personae: Why They Matter and How They Differ Among Heterosexual, Gay and Bisexual Adolescents." *Media Psychology* 21, no. 3, pp. 457–485.

Boorstin, D. 1961. *The Image: A Guide to Pseudo Events in America.* New York, NY: Harper and Row.

Breves, L.P., N. Liebers, M. Abt, and A. Kunze. December 2019. "The Perceived Fit Between Instagram Influencers and the Endorsed Brand: How Influencer-Brand Fit Affects Source Credibility and Persuasive Effectiveness." *Journal of Advertising Research*, pp. 440–454.

Campbell, C., and J.R. Farrell. 2020. "More than Meets the Eye: The Functional Components Underlying Influencer Marketing." *Business Horizons* 63, no. 4, pp. 469–479.

Campbell, C., and P. Grimm. 2019. "The Challenges Native Advertising Poses: Exploring Potential Federal Trade Commission Responses and Identifying Research Needs." *Journal of Public Policy & Marketing* 38, no. 1, pp. 110–123.

Campbell, M., and C. Warren. 2012. "A Risk of Meaning Transfer: Are Negative Associations More Likely to Transfer Than Positive Associations." *Social Influence* 7, no. 3, pp. 172–92.

Carrillat, F., and J. Illicit. 2019. "The Celebrity Capital Life Cycle: A Framework for Future Research Directions on Celebrity Endorsement." *Journal of Advertising* 48, pp. 61–71.

Choi, S., and N. Rifon. 2007. "Who Is the Celebrity in Advertising? Understanding Dimensions of Celebrity Images." *Journal of Popular Culture* 40, no. 2, pp. 302–324.

Choi, S., and N. Rifon. 2012. "It's a Match: The Impact of Congruence Between Celebrity Image and Consumer Ideal Self On Endorsement Effectiveness." *Psychology & Marketing* 29, no. 9, pp. 639–650.

Chung, S., and H. Cho. 2017. "Fostering Para-Social Relationships with Celebrities on Social Media: Implications for Celebrity Endorsements." *Psychology & Marketing* 34, no. 4, pp. 481–495.

Cialdini, R. 2021. *Influence, New and Expanded: The Psychology of Persuasion.* New York, NY: Harper Business.

Cohen, E.L., and W.J. Tyler. 2016. "Examining Perceived Distance and Personal Authenticity as Mediators of the Effects of Ghost-Tweeting on Para-Social Interaction." *Cyberpsychology, Behavior & Social Networking* 19, no. 5, pp. 342–346.

Collings, R. 2021. "Tula Capitalizes on Influencer Marketing, Doubling Sales Year to Date." *Adweek,* www.adweek.com/commerce/tula-capitalizes-on-influencer-marketing-doubling-sales-year-to-date (accessed June 08, 2021).

Collings, R. 2020. "Skincare Gets a Pandemic Boost and Tula's Record Monthly Sales are Proof." *Adweek*, www.adweek.com/commerce/skincare-gets-a-pandemic-boost-and-Tulas-record-monthly-sales-are-proof (accessed June 08, 2021).

De Veirman, M., V. Cauberghe and L. Hudders. 2017. "Marketing through Instagram Influencers: The Impact of Number of Followers and Product Divergence on Brand Attitude." *International Journal of Advertising* 36, no. 5, pp. 798–828.

Delbaere, M., B. Michael and B.J. Phillips. 2021. "Social Media Influencers: A Route to Brand Engagement for Their Followers." *Psychology & Marketing* 38, pp. 101–112.

Djafarova, E., and C. Rushworth. 2017. "Exploring the Credibility of Online Celebrities' Instagram Profiles in Influencing the Purchase Decisions of Young Female Users." *Computers in Human Behavior* 68, pp. 1–7.

Driessens, O. 2013. "The Celebritization of Society and Culture: Understanding the Structural Dynamics of Celebrity Culture." *International Journal of Cultural Studies* 16, no. 3, pp. 641–657.

Eggins, S., and D. Slade. 1997. *Analyzing Casual Conversation.* Washington, DC: Cassell.

Eisend, M., and T. Langner. 2010. "Immediate and Delayed Advertising Effects of Celebrity Endorsers' Attractiveness and Expertise." *International Journal of Advertising* 29, no. 4, pp. 527–546.

Erdogan, B., C. Zafer, M. Baker, and S. Tagg. 2001. "Selecting Celebrity Endorsers: The Practitioner's Perspective." *Journal of Advertising Research* 41, no. 3, pp. 39–48.

Erdogan, B.Z. May, 1999. "Celebrity Endorsements: A Literature Review." *Journal of Marketing Management* 14, pp. 291–314.

Evans, N.J., J. Phua, J. Lim, and H. Jun 2017. "Disclosing Instagram Influencer Advertising: The Effects of Disclosure Language on Advertising Recognition,

Attitudes, and Behavioral Intent." *Journal of Interactive Advertising* 17, no. 2, pp. 138–149.

Feng, Y. 2016. "Are You Connected? Evaluating Information Cascades in Online Discussion about the "RaceTogetherCampaign." *Computers in Human Behavior* 54, pp. 43–53.

Ferchaud, A., J. Grzelso, S. Orme, and J. LaGroue. 2018. "Parasocial Attributes and YouTube Personalities: Exploring Content Trends Across the Most Subscribed YouTube Channels." *Computers in Human Behavior* 80, pp. 88–96.

Freberg, K., K. Graham, K. McGaughey, and L.A. Freberg. 2011. "Who Are the Social Media Influencers? A Study of Public Perceptions of Personality." *Public Relations Review* 37, no. 1, pp. 90–92.

Freeman, K., P. Spencer, and A. Bird. May 23, 2012. "Three Myths about What Customers Want." *Harvard Business Review.* www.hbr.org/2012/05/three-myths-about-customers-eng (accessed July 03, 2021).

Geyser, W. November 10, 2020. "8 Marketing Job Titles for the Skill Sets You Want in Your Growing Marketing Team." *Influencer Marketing Hub.* https://influencermarketinghub.com/marketing-job-titles (accessed May 13, 2021).

Haenlein, M., E. Anadol, T. Farnsworth, H. Hugo, J. Hunichen, and D. Welte. 2020. "Navigating the New Era of Influencer Marketing: How to Be Successful on Instagram, Tik Tok & Co." *California Management Review* 63, no. 1, pp. 5–25.

Harold, C. April 21, 2020. "The Power of Pet Influencers and How to Work with One." *Pet Product News.* www.petproductnews.com/archives/the-power-of-pet-influencers-and-how-to-work-with-one/article_b7cc1905-a04f-55fa-b22a-7001a58035b6.html (accessed June 01, 2021).

Henderson, G. August 24, 2020. "How Much Time Does the Average Person Spend in Social Media." *Digitalmarketing.org.* www.digitalmarketing.org/blog/how-much-time-does-the-average-person-spend-on-social-media (accessed February 10, 2021).

Hiebert, P. February 25, 2021. "The Story Behind Clorox's Mystery Recording Artist." *Adweek.* www.adweek.com/brand-marketing/the-story-behind-cloroxs-mystery-recording-artist-clrx/ (accessed June 01, 2021).

Horton, D., and R.R. Wohl. 1956. "Mass Communication and Para-Social Interaction: Observations On Intimacy at a Distance." *Psychiatry* 19, pp. 185–206.

Hovland, C., I. Janis and H. Kelley. 1953. *Communication and Persuasion.* New Haven, CT: Yale University Press.

Hutcheson, S. January 29, 2019. "Food Blogger Alex Snodgrass of The Defined Dish Shares Recipe for Success." *USA Today.* www.usatoday.com/story/money/careers/career-advice/2019/01/29/defined-dish-how-food-blogger-alex-snodgrass-earned-success/2677627002/ (accessed June 01, 2021).

Iqbal, M. February 10, 2021. "TikTok Revenue and Usage Statistics." *BusinessofApps.* www.businessofapps.com/data/tik-tok-statistics/ (accessed March 10, 2021).

Jin, L. December 17, 2020. "The Creator Economy Needs a Middle Class." *Harvard Business Review.* https://hbr.org/2020/12/the-creator-economy-needs-a-middle-class (accessed February 01, 2021).

Kahle, L.R., and P.M. Homer. 1985. "Physical Attractiveness of the Celebrity Endorser: A Social Adaptation Perspective." *Journal of Consumer Research* 11, no. 4, pp. 954–968.

Kamins, M. March, 1990. "An Investigation into the "Match Up" Hypothesis in Celebrity Advertising: When Beauty May Be Only Skin Deep." *Journal of Advertising* 19, pp. 4–13.

Kapitan, S., and D. Silvera. 2016. "From Digital Influencers to Celebrity Endorsers: Attributions Drive Endorser Effectiveness." *Marketing Letters* 27, no. 3, pp. 553–567.

Katz, E., and P.F. Lazersfeld. 1955. *Personal Influence.* Glenco, IL: The Free Press.

Kaur, T. March 16, 2019. "The Power of Influencer Marketing: Fyre Festival Case Study." *Meltwater.* www.meltwater.com/en/blog/the-power-of-influencer-marketing-fyre-festival-case-study (accessed March 4, 2021).

Kay, S., R. Mulcahy, and J. Parkinson. 2020. "When Less Is More: The Impact of Macro and Micro Social Media Influencers' Disclosure." *Journal of Marketing Management* 36, no. 3–4, pp. 248–278.

Kees, J., and C.J. Andrews. 2019. "Research Issues and Needs at the Intersection of Advertising and Public Policy." *Journal of Advertising* 48, pp. 126–135.

Kelman, H. 1958. "Compliance, Identification and Internationalization: Three Processes of Attitude Change." *Journal of Conflict Resolution* 2, no. 1, pp. 51–60.

Khamis, S., L. Ang and R. Welling. 2016. "Self-Branding 'Microcelebrity' and the Rise of SMIs." *Celebrity Studies,* pp. 1–18.

Kim, J., and H. Song. 2016. "Celebrity's Self-Disclosure on Twitter and Para-Social Relationships: A Mediating Role of Social Presence." *Computers in Human Behavior* 62, pp. 570–577.

Knoll, J., and J. Matthes. 2017. "The Effectiveness of Celebrity Endorsements: A Meta-Analysis." *Journal of the Academy of Marketing Science* 45, pp. 55–75.

Lafferty, B.A., R.E. Goldsmith, and L. Flynn. 2005. "Are Innovators Influenced by Endorser Expertise in an Advertisement When Evaluating a High Technology Product?" *Journal of Marketing Theory and Practice* 13, no. 3, pp. 32–48.

Liefreing, I. March 29, 2018. "Influencers Are Getting Long Term Contracts That Treat Them More Like Traditional Talent." *Digiday.* https://digiday.com/marketing/influencers-getting-long-term-contracts-that-treat-them-more-like-traditional-talent (accessed March 04, 2021).

Lin, H.C., P.F. Bruning, and H. Swarna. 2018. "Using Online Opinion Leaders to Promote the Hedonic and Utilitarian Value of Products and Services." *Business Horizons* 61, pp. 431–442.

Lou, C., and S. Yuan. 2019. "Influencer Marketing: How Message Value and Credibility Affect Consumer Trust of Branded Content on Social Media." *Journal of Interactive Advertising* 19, no. 1, pp. 58–73.

Lynch, J., and D. Schuler. 1994. "The Matchup Effect of Spokesperson and Product Congruency: A Schema Theory Interpretation." *Psychology & Marketing* 11, no. 5, pp. 417–445.

Maltby, J. September 22, 2020. "The Rise of the Creator Economy." *Flybridge*. https://medium.com/@flybridge/the-rise-of-the-creator-economy (accessed June 01, 2021).

McCracken, G. December 1989. "Who Is the Celebrity Endorser Cultural Foundations of the Endorsement Process." *Journal of Consumer Research* 16, pp. 310–320.

McGinnies, E., and C.D. Ward. 1980. "Better liked than Right." *Personality and Social Psychology Bulletin* 6, no. 3, pp. 467–72.

McGuire, W. 1985. "Attitudes and Attitude Change." In *Handbook of Social Psychology*, eds. G. Lindzey and E. Aronson. pp. 233–346, Vol. 2. New York, NY: Random House.

Miller, F., and C.T. Allen. July, 2012. "How Does Celebrity Meaning Transfer? Investigating the Process of Meaning Transfer with Celebrity Affiliates and Mature Brands." *Journal of Consumer Psychology* 22, pp. 443–452.

Monllos, K. February 12, 2021. "The Momentum Is There: In 2021, Marketers Are Starting to See TikTok as a Staple of the Social Budget." *Digiday*. https://digiday.com/marketing/marketers-see-tiktok-as-a-staple-of-the-social-budget/

Murphy, D. February 11, 2020. "How Glossier Built a $1.2 Billion Brand Off the Back of Content." *Privy*. www.privy.com/blog/glossier

N.A October 23, 2019. "Social Media Influencer Jobs." *IZEA,* www.izea.com (accessed May 07, 2021).

N.A. "Top 5 Influencer Marketing Fails: When Influencer Marketing Goes Wrong." *Mediakix*. https://mediakix.com/blog/influencer-marketing-fails

N.A. "6 Influencer Marketing Case Studies including TikTok." *Mediakix*. www.mediakix.com (accessed February 03, 2021).

N.A. "The State of Influencer Marketing 2021." *Linqia*. www.linqia.com (accessed February 08, 2021).

N.A. 2018. "Advertisers Love Influencer Marketing: ANA Study." *Association of National Advertisers*. https://ana.net/content/show/id/48437 (accessed February 10, 2021).

N.A. 2020. "3 Stats That Show Influencers Are as Influential as Ever." *YPulse Daily*. New York, NY: YPulse. (accessed January 10, 2021).

N.A. 2020. "Association of National Advertisers New Report Shows Spending on Content Marketing Climbing Sharply." www.ana.net/content/show/id/pr-2020-spending-climbing (accessed April 10, 2021).

N.A. 2020. "Influencer Marketing Benchmark Report 2020." Influencer Marketing Hub. www.influencermarketinghub.com/influencer-marketing-benchmark-report-2020 (accessed April 01, 2021).

N.A. 2020. "The Influencer Report: Engaging Gen Z and Millennials." *Morning Consult*. www.morningconsult.com (accessed June 01, 2021).

N.A. 2021. "2018 State of the Creator Economy." *IZEA*. www.izea.com

N.A. 2021. "B2B Influencer Marketing Guide." IZEA. www.izea.com (accessed July 01, 2021).

N.A. 2021. "Dunkin Donuts" in 6 Influencer Marketing Case Studies Including TikTok from MediaKix." www.mediakix.com (accessed April 02, 2021).

N.A. 2021. "Influencer Marketing Benchmark Report 2020." *Influencer Marketing Hub*. www.influencermarketinghub.com/influencer-marketing-benchmark-report-2020 (accessed April 01, 2021).

N.A. 2021. "Influencer Marketing Statistics Every Marketer Needs to Know." *Mediakix*. https://mediakix.com/influencer-marketing-resources/influencer-marketing-statistics/ (accessed June 01, 2021).

N.A. 2021. "Influencer Typology" *Mediakix*. www.mediakix.com (accessed June 01, 2021).

N.A. 2021. "The Differences between Brand Ambassadors, Influencers, and Celebrities." *Mediakix*. https://mediakix.com/blog/brand-ambassadors-influencers-celebrities (accessed June 01, 2021).

N.A. 2021. "The Rise of Dermtok." *Glossy*. www.glossy.co/beauty/the-rise-of-dermtok/ (accessed July 02, 2021).

N.A. 2021. "The State of Influencer Marketing 2021." *Linqia*. www.linqia.com (accessed June 01, 2021).

N.A. 2021. "Top 5 Influencer Marketing Fails: When Influencer Marketing Goes Wrong." *Mediakix*. https://mediakix.com/blog/influencer-marketing-fails (accessed June 30, 2021).

N.A. 2021. "What Constitutes an Influencer?" *Mediakix*. https://mediakix.com/blog/influencer-definition-marketing (accessed June 01, 2021).

N.A. 2021. "What Is Content Marketing?" *Content Marketing Institute*. https://contentmarketinginstitute.com/what-is-content-marketing (accessed March 02, 2021).

N.A. 2021. IZEA "2018 State of the Creator Economy." www.izea.com (accessed April 23, 2021).

N.A. 2021. IZEA Customer Stories "Commonwealth of Kentucky." www. Izea. com (accessed July 01, 2021).

N.A. 2021."Not Another State of Marketing Report 2020." *Hubspot*. www.hubspot.com/state-of-marketing (accessed January 08, 2021).

N.A. April 22, 2021. "13 Influencer Marketing Trends to Watch in 2021." *Influencer Marketing Hub*. https://influencermarketinghub.com/influencer-marketing-trends-to-watch-in-2021 (accessed July 01, 2021).

N.A. April 22, 2021. "13 Influencer Marketing Trends to Watch in 2021." *Influencer Marketing Hub*. https://influencermarketinghub.com/influencer-marketing-trends (accessed May 08, 2021).

N.A. August 19, 2019. "Marketing to Generation Z." *WP Engine*. https://wpengine.com/resources/marketing-to-gen-z/ (accessed June 01, 2021).

N.A. December 04, 2013. "IAB: The Native Advertising Playbook." *Interactive Advertising Bureau*. www.iab.com (accessed July 03, 2021).

N.A. February 08, 2019. "From Fans to Nano Influencers, a look at the evolution of influencer marketing, TFL. www.thefashionlaw.com/fans-and-micro-micro-influencers-the-answer-to-growing/ (accessed July 02, 2021).

N.A. January 2021. "2021 State of Influencer Equality." *IZEA*. www.izea.com

N.A. January 2021. "Influencer Marketing for the Covid Vaccine." IZEA. www.IZEA.com

N.A. July 20, 2021. "US Influencer Spending Expected to Surpass $3 billion in 2021." *eMarketer*, www.emarketer.com/content/us-influencer-spending-surpass-3-billion-2021 (accessed July 24, 2021).

N.A. July 20, 2021. "US Influencer Spending Expected to Surpass $3 billion in 2021." *eMarketer*. (accessed July 24, 2021). www.emarketer.com/content/us-influencer-spending-surpass-3-billion-2021

N.A. June 12, 2019. "Mobile Fact Sheet." *Pew Research*. www.pewresearch.org/internet/fact-sheet/mobile/ (accessed June 01, 2021).

N.A. May 05, 2021. "What Is a Creator and How to Improve Your Content Creation Skills." *Influencer Marketing Hub*. https:influencermarketinghub.com/what-is-a-creator (accessed June 20, 2021).

N.A. May 13, 2021. "Creator Earnings Benchmark Report" *Influencer Marketing Hub*, https://influencermarketing hub.com/creator-earnings-benchmark-report (accessed June 09, 2021).

N.A. May 15, 2021. "The Creator Economy Landscape: Examining an Economy That's Changing the World." *Influencer Marketing Hub*. https://influencermarketinghub.com/creator-economy-landscape/ (accessed June 09, 2021).

N.A. September 23, 2020. "What Is the Creator Economy?" *Influencer Marketing Hub*. https://influencermarketinghub.com/creator-economy (accessed February 20, 2021).

N.A. September 23, 2020. "What is the Creator Economy?" *Influencer Marketing Hub*. https://influencermarketinghub.com/creator-economy (accessed February 10, 2021).

Nguyen, A. December 08, 2020. "Using Influencer Marketing to Defend the Causes You Care About" *Upfluence*. www.unfluence.com/influence-marketing/causes-nonprofits (accessed June 01, 2021).

Ohanian, R. 1990. "Construction and Validation of a Scale to Measure Celebrity Endorsers' Perceived Expertise, Trustworthiness and Attractiveness." *Journal of Advertising* 19, no. 3, pp. 39–52.

Ohanian, R. February/March, 1991. "The Impact of Celebrity Spokespersons' Perceived Image on Consumers Intention to Purchase." *Journal of Advertising Research* 31, pp. 46–54.

Pavlovskaya, E. April 20, 2021. "71 Up-To-Date YouTube Statistics for Your Marketing Strategy in 2021." *SEMRush Blog.* www.semrush.com/blog/youtube-stats/ (accessed May 25, 2021).

Planos, J. June 08, 2021. "Student-Athletes Will soon be Social Media Influencers. And one College Program is helping them do it." *FiveThirtyEight.* https://fivethirtyeight.com/features/student-athletes-will-soon-be-social-media-influencers-and-one-college-program-is-helping-them-do-it (accessed July 09, 2021).

Princewall, T.K. April 08, 2021. "Is the 2020s the Decade of the Creator Economy?" www.medium.com/swlh/is-the-2020s-the-decade-of-the-creator-economy (accessed July 01, 2021).

Quesenberry, K. 2020. *Social Media Strategy: Marketing, Advertising, and Public Relations in the Consumer Revolution,* 3rd ed. New York, NY: Roman & Littlefield.

Rimmer, K. n.d. "The Stats Driving Influencer Marketing 2019." *Tribe.* https://tribegroup.co/blog/the-stats-driving-influencer-marketing-in-2019 (accessed March 10, 2021).

Riot Games. June 29, 2021. *How We Blew Up Our Influencer Strategy to Launch the Next Massive Game with Ali Miller, Global Influencer Program Lead, Riot Games.* AdWeek Social Media Week LA.

Rourke, L., T. Anderson, D.R. Garrison, and W. Archer. 2001. "Assessing Social Presence in Asynchronous Text-Based Computer Conferencing." *Journal of Distance Education* 14, pp. 1–8.

Russell, A. 2020. *The Influencer Code: How to Unlock the Power of Influencer Marketing.* Hatherleigh Press.

Sander, E. March 26, 2021. "Cetaphil sees Dermatologists as Key to Gen Z Popularity." *Glossy.* www.glossy.co/beauty/cetaphil-sees-dermatologists-as-key-to-Gen-Z-popularity

Schaffer, N. 2020. *The Age of Influence: The Power of Influencers to Elevate your Brand.* New York, NY: HarperCollins Leadership.

Schimmelpfennig, C., and J.B. Hunt. 2020. "Fifty Years of Celebrity Endorser Research: Support for a Comprehensive Celebrity Endorsement Strategy Framework." *Psychology & Marketing* 37, no. 3, pp. 488–503.

Schimmelpfennig, C., and J.B. Hunt. 2020. "Fifty Years of Celebrity Endorser Research: Support for a Comprehensive Celebrity Endorsement Strategy Framework." *Psychology* & *Marketing* 37, no. 3, pp. 488–503.

Schouten, A.P., L. Janssen, and M. Verspaget. 2020. "Celebrity vs. Influencer Endorsements in Advertising: The Role of Identification, Credibility, and Product-Endorser Fit." *International Journal of Advertising* 39, no. 2, pp. 258–281.

Schram, R. 2020. "The State of the Creator Economy." *Journal of Brand Strategy* 9, no. 2, pp. 152–162.

Shaffer, N. 2020. *Age of Influence: The Power of Influencers to Elevate Your Brand.* New York, NY: HarperCollins Leadership.

Siemens, J., S. Smith, D. Fisher, and T.D. Jensen. 2018. "Product Expertise Versus Professional Expertise: Congruency Between and Endorsers Chosen Profession and the Endorsed Product." *Journal of Targeting, Measurement and Analysis for Marketing* 16, no. 3, pp. 159–168.

Solis, B. "Influence 2.0: The Future of Influencer Marketing." Altimeter@ Prophet. www.influencermarketinghub.com (accessed January 07, 2021).

Stevenson, S. March 29, 2021. "Peloton Won the Pandemic. Can it Survive the Reopening of Gyms?" *Slate.* https://slate.com/business/2021/03/peloton-pandemic-sales

Taylor, C.R. 2021. "The Urgent Need for More Research on Influencer Marketing." *International Journal of Advertising* 39, no. 7, pp. 889–891.

Thimothy, S. May 05, 2021. "The New Creator Economy: What Entrepreneurs Can Expect." *Fast Company.* www.fastcompany.com/90633385/the-new-creator-economy (accessed July 01, 2021).

Thomas, V.L., and K. Fowler. 2021. "Close Encounters of the AI Kind: Use of AI Influencers as Brand Endorsers. *Journal of Advertising* 50, no. 1, pp. 11–25.

Till, B.D., and M. Busler. 1998. "Matching Products with Endorsers: Attractiveness Versus Expertise." *Journal of Consumer Marketing* 15, no. 6, pp. 576–586.

Tobin, J. 2019. "Three Influencer Marketing Problems That Brands Themselves Can Be Created." *Forbes.* www.forbes.com/sites/forbesagencycouncil/2019/10/14/three-influencer-marekting-problems-that-brands-themselves-have-created/ (accessed April 04, 2021).

Torres, P., M. Augusto, and M. Matos. 2019. "Antecedents and Outcomes of Digital Influencer Endorsement: An Exploratory Study." *Psychology* & *Marketing* 36, pp. 1267–1276.

Tu, C. 2020. "Online Learning Migration: From Social Learning Theory to Social Presence Theory in a CMC Environment." *Journal of Network and Computer Applications* 23, no. 9, pp. 27–37.

Valsesia, F., D. Proserpio, and J. Nunes. 2020. "The Positive Effect of Not Following Others on Social Media." *Journal of Marketing Research* 57, no. 6, pp. 1152–1168.

Van Dijk, K.N. July 09, 2020. "Glossier Case Study: A Digital Beauty Brand." https://advertikmedia.com/glossier-case-study-a-digital-beauty-brand (accessed July 01, 2021).

Vaughan, C. March 29, 2016. "Influencer Marketing Update: Non-Celebrity Influencers 10 Times more Likely to Drive In-Store Purchases." *Collectivebias. com.* https://collectivebias.com/blog/2016/03/influencer-marketing-update-non-celebrity-influencers-10-times-likely-drive-store-purchases/

Voorveld, H.A.M. 2019. "Brand Communication in Social Media: A Research Agenda." *Journal of Advertising* 48, pp. 14–26.

Wang, S.W., and A.C. Scheinbaum. 2018. "Enhancing Brand Credibility Via Celebrity Endorsement." *Journal of Advertising Research* 58, no. 1, pp. 16–32.

Wilde, K. January 11, 2020. "6 Marketing Lessons from Glossier." *Better Marketing,* https://bettermarketing.pub/6-marketing-lessons-from-glossier (accessed March 04, 2021).

Wojdynski, B.W., and N.J. Evans. 2016. "Going Native: Effects of Disclosure Position and Language on the Recognition and Evaluation of Online Native Advertising." *Journal of Advertising* 46, no. 2, pp. 1–12.

Wong, V.C., H. Fock, and C. Ho. 2020. "Toward a Process-Transfer Model of the Endorser Effect." *Journal of Marketing Research* 57, no. 3, pp. 565–581.

Wurmser, Y. May 30, 2019. "US Time Spent with Mobile 2019." *eMarketer.* www.emarketer.com/content/us-time-spent-with-mobilie-2019 (accessed March 01, 2021).

Yang, P. December 20, 2020. "Creator Hierarchy of Needs." *Creator Economy.* https://creatoreconomy.so/p/creator-hierarchy-of-needs (accessed March 09, 2021).

Yang, P. May 24, 2020. "Creator Demand Curve." *Creator Economy.* https://creatoreconomy.so/p/creator-demand-curve (accessed February 09, 2021).

Young, L. February 26, 2020. "Blue Apron: 3 Ingredients for the Perfect Influencer Campaign." *Klear.* https://klear.com/blog/blue-apron-3-ingredients-for-the-perfect-influencer-campaign (accessed June 30, 2021).

Yuan, S., and C. Lou. 2020. "How Social Media Influencers Foster Relationships with Followers: The Roles of Source Credibility and Fairness in Para-Social Relationship and Product Interest." *Journal of Interactive Advertising* 20, no. 2, pp. 133–147.

Yuan, Y., and J. Constine. "*Signal Fire's Creator Economy Market Map.*" *Signal Fire Blog.* https://signalfire.com/blog/creator-economy/ (accessed March 03, 2021).

About the Author

Stacy Landreth Grau, PhD, is a professor of entrepreneurship and innovation practice at the Neeley School of Business at Texas Christian University (TCU) and Director, IdeaFactory in the School of Interdisciplinary Studies at TCU. Previously, she spent 10 years of teaching in the marketing department at TCU where she researched endorsers and source expertise as well as the digital and social media marketing, particularly social media influencers. She developed several courses around digital and social media marketing, marketing communications, and design thinking. Stacy also has worked with several integrated marketing communications firms as a research consultant as well as marketing consultant in the fitness industry. For more information, visit the website at www.creator-nation.com

Index

OTHER TITLES IN THE DIGITAL AND SOCIAL MEDIA MARKETING AND ADVERTISING COLLECTION

Naresh Malhotra, Georgia Tech, Editor

- *Stand Out!!* by Brian McGurk
- *Super Sonic Logos* by David Allan
- *The Digital Marketing Landscape* by Jessica Rogers
- *Marketing in the Digital World* by Avinash Kapoor
- *Digital Marketing Management, Second Edition* by Debra Zahay
- *Make Your Nonprofit Social* by Lindsay Chambers, Jennifer Morehead, and Heather Sallee
- *Make Your Business Social* by Lindsay Chambers, Jennifer Morehead, and Heather Sallee
- *Social Media Marketing, Second Edition* by Emi Moriuchi
- *Tell Me About Yourself* by Stavros Papakonstantinidis

Concise and Applied Business Books

The Collection listed above is one of 30 business subject collections that Business Expert Press has grown to make BEP a premiere publisher of print and digital books. Our concise and applied books are for...

- Professionals and Practitioners
- Faculty who adopt our books for courses
- Librarians who know that BEP's Digital Libraries are a unique way to offer students ebooks to download, not restricted with any digital rights management
- Executive Training Course Leaders
- Business Seminar Organizers

Business Expert Press books are for anyone who needs to dig deeper on business ideas, goals, and solutions to everyday problems. Whether one print book, one ebook, or buying a digital library of 110 ebooks, we remain the affordable and smart way to be business smart. For more information, please visit www.businessexpertpress.com, or contact sales@businessexpertpress.com.

www.ingramcontent.com/pod-product-compliance
Lightning Source LLC
Chambersburg PA
CBHW061314220326
41599CB00026B/4876